D1592120

The Power of "One"

"Cast in Stone"

The distinguished roll of inclusion in the Automotive Hall of Fame now numbers 217 individuals ranging from large-company founders such as Henry Ford to lone-eagle entrepreneurs and inventors like Ralph R. Teetor. All share the common denominator of significant contribution to the automobile industry over their lifetime and exhibiting the highest levels of individual courage and tenacity.

The Automotive Hall of Fame is not just about the recognition and remembrance of the distinguished individuals that have made momentous strides and contributions to the industry. While that's important as a function of archival history, perhaps the most important contribution the institution makes is the offering of inspiration and encouragement, provided for future achievers with the details of the pioneering provenance of the current honored members.

The media would lead you to believe that we are without industry heroes and individuals worthy of emulation. The Automotive Hall of Fame stands as a solid contradiction to this line of thinking, offering a balance of outstanding individuals from a wide variety of disciplines that applied their energies and ingenuity to achieve greatness in the field.

The automotive industry is a prime testament to the worldwide achievements of individuals driven by dreams, desire, and awareness of needs; to invent, refine and develop not only vehicles and accessories but also the support and marketing systems necessary to maintain the vital and growing culture of global transportation.

> *"The foundation of all excellence in action, intellectual and physical, is laid in self-control: In which the passions and desires are hushed, and the intellect, undisturbed in the silence and solitude of thoughts, pursues her way and reaches the desired conclusion."*
>
> -H. L. Baugher-

As a nation, we need to re-invigorate and re-inspire. Just as with the Sputnik renaissance in the '60s that led to men walking on the moon, we need a kindred awakening that places appropriately high values on learning. We obviously need a decided shift in the priorities of "being cool" that results in placing knowledge and viable skills on a higher order than hip-hop's "gangsta" culture.

The automotive industry was not built by the tired, timid, uninspired or uninformed, nor will it be re-invigorated by similar traits. I firmly believe that the models of entrepreneurial courage necessary for the tasks at hand are within our grasp. In fact, 217 such examples are for the asking—at the Automotive Hall of Fame.

Drive in Peace

Gerry Durnell
Editor & Publisher

Automobile Quarterly

The Connoisseur's Publication of Motoring
– *Today, Yesterday, and Tomorrow* –

GERRY DURNELL
Editor & Publisher

KAYE BOWLES-DURNELL
Associate Publisher

JOHN C. DURNELL
Chief Operations Officer, Technical Editor

TRACY POWELL
Managing Editor

JOHN EVANS
Chief Financial Officer

DAN BULLEIT
Art Director

ROD HOTTLE
Administrative Assistant

ROBIN JEFFERS
Customer Service

L. SCOTT BAILEY
Founding Editor and Publisher

Contributing Photographers
PHIL BERG
ROY STRYKER

Contributing Writers
RANDY BARNETT
PHIL BERG
FRED BOOTH
GRIFFITH BORGESON
JEFFREY GODSHALL
CARL GOODWIN
ALISON TARTT

www.autoquarterly.com

ISBN 1-59613-053-9
(978-1-59613-053-1)

Printed in Korea

Contents

VOLUME 47, NUMBER 1 • FIRST QUARTER 2007

Cover: "Senna" 20 x 30 inches.

Left: "Turn 13" 20 x 30 inches.

LaSalle
The Cadillac Companion

Against a century-old record of successful competition, Cadillac is obliged to recognize its one failure—the warmly remembered LaSalle. Despite a promising beginning, despite generally brilliant styling and obvious high quality, despite determined efforts to make the car a success, the LaSalle slipped quietly out of production in the summer of 1940, its passing scarcely noted by the automotive press. LaSalle's beginnings, however, were far more dramatic, stretching back 20 years earlier.

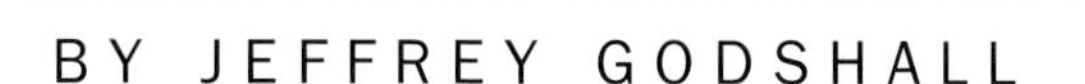

BY JEFFREY GODSHALL

The sharp economic recession of 1920-21 had a profound effect on the automobile industry and on the General Motors Corporation in particular. In the 1920 panic William C. Durant lost control of GM for a second and final time and left the corporation to begin again with his own Durant Motors. When he left, GM was a polyglot of unrelated companies with little central control and a confused product lineup. GM cars garnered only 12 percent of the 1921 U.S. market, compared with Ford's 60 percent, and the situation was becoming critical. In April of that year the GM Executive Committee set up a special committee of the Advisory Staff, headed by Alfred P. Sloan, Jr., to study the corporation's product policies. From that study came a report that would have far-reaching results. Sloan found that only Buick and Cadillac were established, money-making automobiles. The rest of the line was shaky at best and some, like Sheridan and Scripps-Booth, were real dogs. Sloan made plans to improve all lines and introduce new products where necessary, so that GM would have a competitive car line in every price class.

The 1927 LaSalle was a styling *coup,* the first mass-produced automobile designed from "stem to stern"—as Harley Earl noted—by a designer. The LaSalle was intended as Cadillac's "companion car," filling the gap between the top-priced Buick 6 and the cheapest Cadillac.

Sloan's study indicated that a car was clearly needed to fill the $1,000 gap between Buick and Cadillac, and in 1924 he requested Cadillac to study the possibility of producing a family-type car to sell around $2,000. At the time Cadillac was progressing in a steady but unremarkable fashion, clearly established as a leader in the high-priced field yet lagging behind Packard. Since the proposed new car was to be a quality product and since Cadillac production volume could stand a shot in the arm, Cadillac was a logical choice to build the new car. When Lawrence P. Fisher assumed the general managership of the Cadillac Motor Car Company in 1925, one of his first programs was the inauguration of a $5 million expansion program that increased Cadillac production capacity to 60,000 cars annually in anticipation of the division's forthcoming entry into a lower-priced field.

So it was that Cadillac embarked on the design and manufacture of a junior edition of the "Standard of the World." The choice of a suitable name was no difficulty. Since Cadillac itself was named in honor of Antoine de la Mothe Cadillac, founder of Detroit in 1701, the choice of another explorer's name to grace the new car was indeed appropriate. That explorer was Rene Robert Cavelier, Sieur de la Salle, who claimed all of Louisiana for King Louis XIV of France in 1682. Unfortunately, the explorer LaSalle came to a sudden end, killed by his own men while leading a disastrous march through east Texas in 1687. Considering the subsequent career of the LaSalle automobile, the name choice was unknowingly prophetic.

Yet the birth of the LaSalle was an event of considerable pleasure for Cadillac and of lasting significance for the automotive industry. Introduced in March 1927, the LaSalle emerged as a companion to the prestigious Cadillac, aimed at the owner-driver as a man looking for an automobile of high quality and unquestioned value in a smaller, less expensive, more maneuverable package. No effort was made to conceal the LaSalle's Cadillac heritage and the car was unabashedly advertised as a "blood brother to the Cadillac" and of "genuine Cadillac caliber." The hoped-for target of $2,000 was not reached, but at $2,495 to $2,685, the LaSalle slipped neatly between the most expensive Buick ($1,995) and the cheapest Cadillac ($2,995). The price class the LaSalle was entering included some tough

competition, namely the Chrysler Imperial 80, Elcar 8-90, Franklin 11-B, Hupmobile E, Jordan Great Line 8, Kissel 8-75, the little Marmon, Packard 6, Paige 8-85, Peerless 6-72, and the Roamer 8-88.

As nearly everyone knows, the LaSalle was the first production car to be designed by a stylist, and that stylist was Harley Earl. Earl grew up with his father's coach and carriage business in the years leading up to World War I. He was serving as draftsman and later as designer while still in his teens, conjuring up lavish and bizarre coachwork for the likes of "Fatty" Arbuckle and Tom Mix. After the war, Earl Carriage Works was purchased by the Don Lee organization, also of Los Angeles, and Earl was put in charge of the elaborate customizing and coachbuilding works. Earl now rapidly began to make a name for himself.

By the mid-1920s his fame had spread to Detroit, attracting the attention of Lawrence Fisher who was aware that many of Earl's successful designs had appeared on a Cadillac chassis. Fisher was impressed with Earl's approach to car design. Among his innovations was the use of modeling clay to develop the forms of the diverse components. In some of his creations Earl was also designing the complete automobile, molding the hood, fenders, lights and other ingredients into a unified whole rather than a collection of unrelated parts.

Fortunately for Earl and Cadillac, the LaSalle was a handsome automobile indeed. There was a strong Hispano-Suiza look about the car (even to the winged radiator emblem), reflecting Earl's knowledge and appreciation of the most advanced of European design. Until the LaSalle arrived on the scene, most American cars were heavy and clumsy-looking, square-cornered and somewhat overbearing. The LaSalle, with its smooth hood sides and graceful tablespoon fenders, was a move away from the heaviness and toward the fleetness and grace of the mid-classic era. Detailing was equally impressive with a high, handsome radiator, headlamps mounted on vertical stanchions, and side windows on sedans re-proportioned for a fleeter look. Corners were smoothed off wherever possible, and on some cars the hood and cowl were painted a darker shade than the bodies for a unique look. The result was an impressively styled car of unrivaled appeal to quality buyers.

Customers had a choice of 11 body types in the standard line. Eight of these—the two-passenger roadster, coupe and convertible coupe; the four-passenger phaeton, dual-cowl phaeton, and victoria; and the five-passenger sedan and town sedan—were mounted over a 125-inch wheelbase, seven inches shorter

Earl (behind the wheel) and Lawrence Fisher in front of the Copley Plaza Hotel during the 1927 Boston Automobile Show, where the LaSalle was introduced.

than the smallest Cadillac. Three special bodies—a seven-passenger sedan, Imperial sedan and five-passenger Imperial sedan—came on a larger 134-inch chassis. All came with Fisher bodies. Also available was a series of Fleetwood styles for those with more demanding tastes, including a two-passenger coupe and five-passenger sedan, two cabriolet and transformable town cabriolet. The LaSalle represented good value. A dual-cowl phaeton with folding rear tonneau windshield, searchlight, six-wheel equipment with fenderwells, and a dashing appearance (to say nothing of Cadillac quality) could be had for under $3,000.

LaSalle introductory year was a year of sensational happenings, one of which was Charles Lindbergh's solo flight across the Atlantic. Lindbergh and his LaSalle: the perfect photo op.

In engineering the new LaSalle was essentially a lighter, smaller Cadillac. Its 90-degree L-head V-8 had a 3 1/8-inch bore and a 4 15/16-inch stroke. Total displacement was 303 cubic inches; brake horsepower, 75. The 90-degree V-8 was introduced by Cadillac in 1914 and refined and developed down the years. Thus the new car benefited from the parent company's experience gained in building more than 250,000 V-8 engines. The LaSalle engine was quite different, however, from the Cadillac's, being a completely fresh design, which, in a larger-displacement and bigger-bore version, was introduced later in 1927 as the new 341 series Cadillac.

With the new engine, the LaSalle's connecting rod big ends were placed side by side for each pair of cylinders, a major departure from the interlaced forks used by Cadillac until then. The three crankshaft bearings were 2 3/8 inches in diameter. Interchangeable bronze-backed, babbitt-lined, split bushings were used for main bearings. Connecting rods were 10 inches long between centers and the big-end bearings were cast in. Unlike the previous design, which placed cylinders in left and right banks opposite each other and used a forked connected rod on one side, the new layout moved the right bank of cylinders forward 1 3/8 inches and placed two connecting rods side by side on the same crank pin. The detachable cylinder heads were ribbed for "cooling," a neat touch, actually for appearance.

There were two Morse silent chains forward, driven from sprockets on the crankshaft. One drove the centrally located camshaft, situated on the V of the engine directly over the crankshaft. The other chain drove the water pump and generator.

The single-unit carburetor was Cadillac designed and built, located between the manifolds and carrying a raised "LaS" emblem. Fuel was fed to the carburetor from a vacuum tank, a devilish device remembered well by our forefathers. Vacuum from the intake manifold was supplied to a vertical cylinder that induced gasoline to flow from the fuel tank at the rear of the car. Its advantages were complete independence from

Compared to other GM cars, the LaSalle was a more integrated design, with few sharp corners and lines that flowed.

mechanical and electrical failure, but it was apt to go thirsty on a long uphill climb, when manifold vacuum dropped to the vanishing point. LaSalle sought to overcome this fault by incorporating a supplementary vacuum pump driven from an eccentric on the camshaft, which worked much in the same way the auxiliary vacuum pump on a latter-day mechanical fuel pump operates. A one-way valve was included in the system to make sure that the pump's efforts were confined to the vacuum tank.

The Delco ignition system featured a dual-point distributor with centrifugal spark advance, which Cadillac engineers claimed made the steering-wheel spark adjuster unnecessary, so that control was moved to the instrument panel. It was to be used only during hard cranking or when anti-knock gasoline was unavailable, when the car had the optional high compression head.

Engine temperature was controlled by external shutters that were operated by a thermostat in the header tank. Thermostatic temperature control was pioneered by Cadillac in 1914 in its first V-8. The advantage over the internal-thermostat, open-radiator system was that the entire cooling system, including the coolant in the radiator, was kept above freezing temperature during winter months. Cooling-system capacity was five gallons, and airflow through the radiator core was ensured by a six-blade, 20-inch fan.

Lubrication was conventional; connecting-rod bearings were pressure-lubricated through a drilled crankshaft, and the timing chains were oiled by the overflow from the oil-pressure regulator. One feature that was new at the time was the provision for lubricating the valve stem from small oil passages extending from the cylinder walls.

Braking was accomplished by two independent systems much in vogue today, though their actuation was by mechanical means as GM (and Ford) were still somewhat uneasy over the possible consequences of hydraulic line failure. The front shoes were internal expanding while external bands contracted about the rear drums. The handbrake operated through internal shoes on the rear drums only. This arrangement was identical to the Cadillac braking system. The conservative policy of remaining with mechanical brakes was perhaps unjustified, since other makes like Peerless, Reo, Paige and Chrysler Corporation had switched to hydraulics. Indeed it was not until seven years after its introduction that LaSalle was finally to get hydraulics.

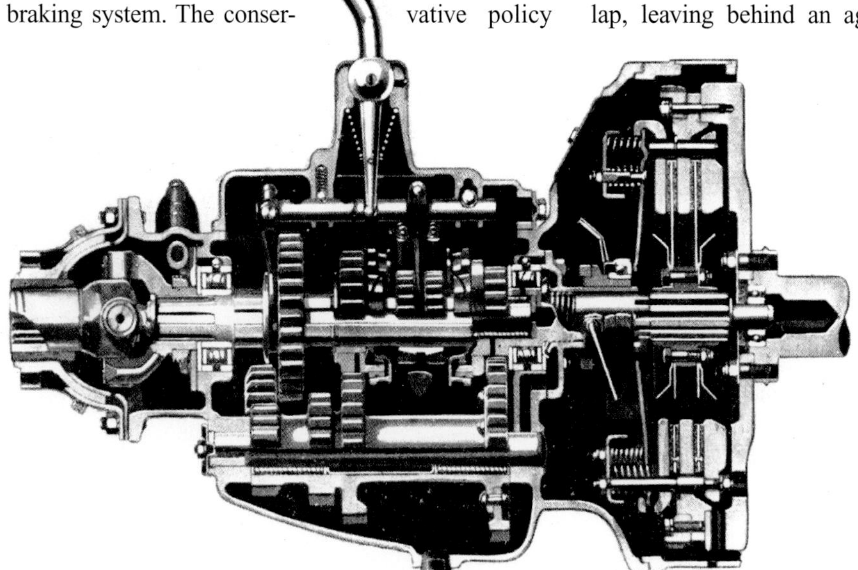

High Performance

It would be a mistake to conclude that the LaSalle, for all its staid heritage and engineering, was an uninspired performer. Three months after its introduction a standard production roadster was taken out to the 3.78-mile track at the GM Proving Ground for a little high-speed work. Fenders and running boards were removed, along with the windshield and headlamps. A slightly higher compression ratio, a hotter camshaft, and a longer rear axle were the only mechanical alterations—but they were enough to reduce a lot of impressionable newsmen to open-mouthed astonishment. "Big Bill" Rader of the Cadillac experimental group and ex-dirt track racer Gus Bell were to serve as driver and riding mechanic.

The test run began at 6:30 a.m., as the little roadster stormed off into its first lap, leaving behind an agglomeration of spare wheels, tires, fuel, mechanics, timekeepers and hopeful GM executives, including Harley Earl. Within a few minutes the hopes of all were to be realized beyond their wildest dreams. Rader was lapping the track in the high 90s and hitting well over 100 mph each time around. It seemed unthinkable that a harmless little touring car could survive this kind of treatment for long.

Soon the first stop for fuel and tire inspection was due, and Rader slid the car to a halt as mechanics swarmed over it. A Cadillac bulletin described it thus:

"Comes the drone of the LaSalle as it roars up to the pits. The car stops, but the engine is kept 'reving,' the corps of mechanics rush each to his appointed task. Water in, gasoline filled, oil replenished simultaneously with the jacking up of the car; off comes the old wheel and on with the new—a drink of water for

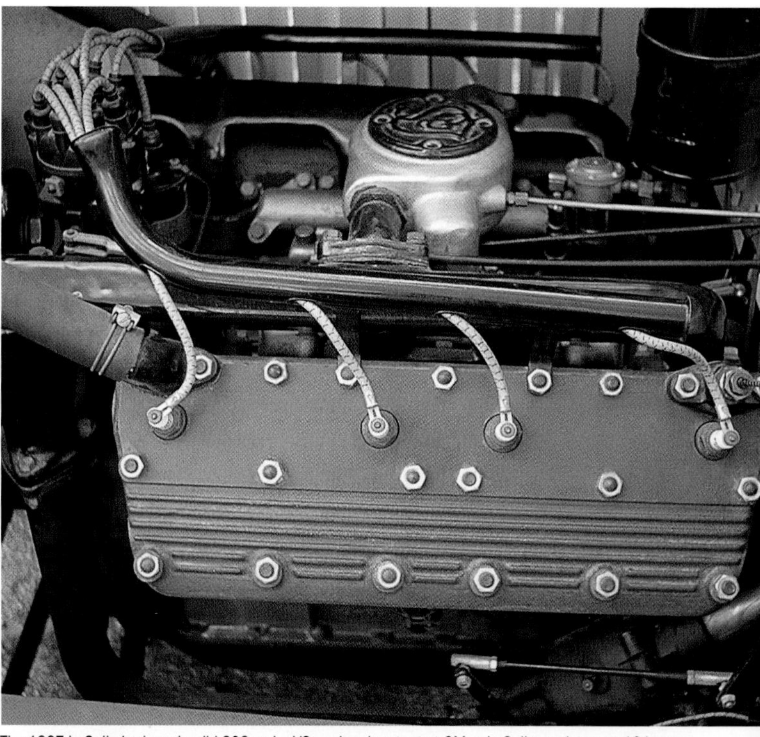

The 1927 LaSalle had a splendid 303 cu.in. V8 engine. In a test at GM, a LaSalle roadster ran 10 hours at an average 95.2 mph, almost as fast as that year's Indy 500 winner. Left: Cutaway of Cadillac's silent Syncro-Mesh transmission, seen in LaSalle models of 1929.

'Big Bill' Rader, face blackened with grime and dust. Ready? Let her go. Engine accelerates with a roar, clutch goes in, wheels shriek and skid violently, and she's off again like a shot from a gun."

Rader made nine such stops and covered 951.9 miles at an amazing average of 95.3 mph before an oil line fractured and put an end to the run after 10 hours. The figures speak plainly enough for themselves, but they become downright uncanny when one considers that the 1927 Indianapolis 500 was won by a 160hp Duesenberg at a mere 2 mph faster—and over half the distance.

And LaSalle stamina was not reserved solely for the racetrack. In another remarkable test of LaSalle qual-

LaSalle soon became a car in its own right, offering Cadillac qualities in a smaller package at a lower price. Above: 1929 LaSalle 328 convertible coupe.

ity, 12 cars were picked at random from the production line and driven over 300,000 miles during a four-month period at the Proving Ground. To everyone's surprise not a single failure of a major component was recorded.

Beautiful lines, great performance and a quality-car heritage made this first LaSalle a real winner, and the public responded by taking 26,807 of the 1927-28 Model 303. During the first year of LaSalle production, Cadillac was obliged to build nearly 21,000 more cars than it had ever built before during any single model year. Cadillac and Sloan and Earl had good reason to be highly pleased with their new baby.

Part of this success may be attributed to the efforts of one Captain Edward V. Rickenbacker, who joined General Motors on Jan. 1, 1928, as a sales "troubleshooter" for Cadillac-LaSalle. One of his accomplishments was the upgrading of Cadillac-LaSalle dealerships whose service departments were, in Captain Eddie's words, "in awful shape. Garages were dirty, the tools lying around everywhere. This slackness frequently spread throughout the entire operation." Improvements were promptly undertaken.

With LaSalle selling so well only minor changes appeared on the 1928 model. Hood sides were changed to accept 28 smaller vertical louvers, replacing the 12 coarser louvers of 1927. As with any successful automotive product, there was the inevitable urge to expand the line and Cadillac succumbed. Three additional models were offered in the standard LaSalle range, including five- and seven-passenger family sedans and a four-passenger coupe, all of which was accompanied by an average $155 price reduction. The Fleetwood line was greatly enlarged to include a four-passenger victoria, two-passenger business coupe, five- and seven-passenger Imperial sedans, and a five-passenger sedan and fixed transformable. Apparently Cadillac felt the day of the small, high-quality luxury car had really arrived.

One advantage in having a fine car like Cadillac as a sponsor was that when Cadillac engineers came up with any significant improvements the LaSalle was quick to benefit. So in 1929 LaSalle quietly adopted Cadillac's silent Syncro-Mesh transmission, introduced on the parent car a year earlier. The "Clashless Syncro-

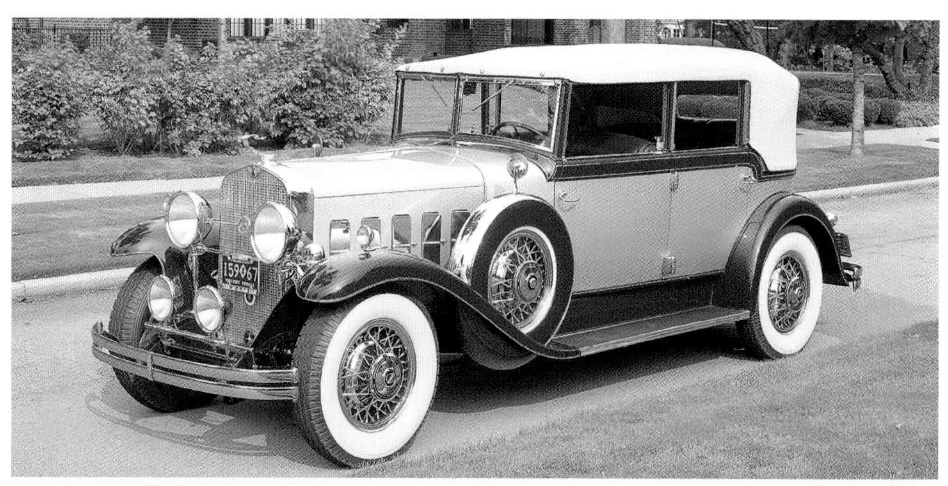

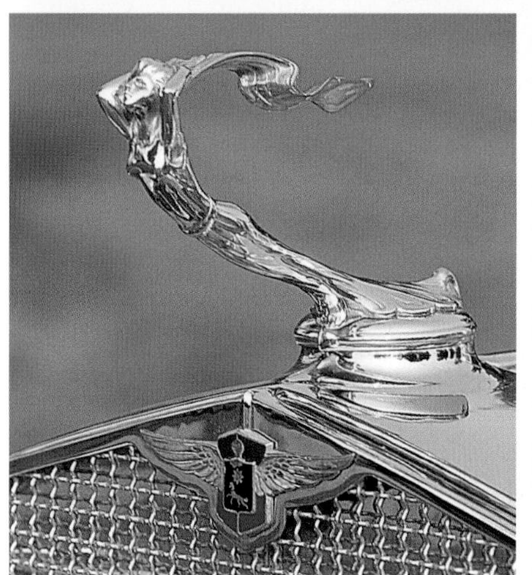

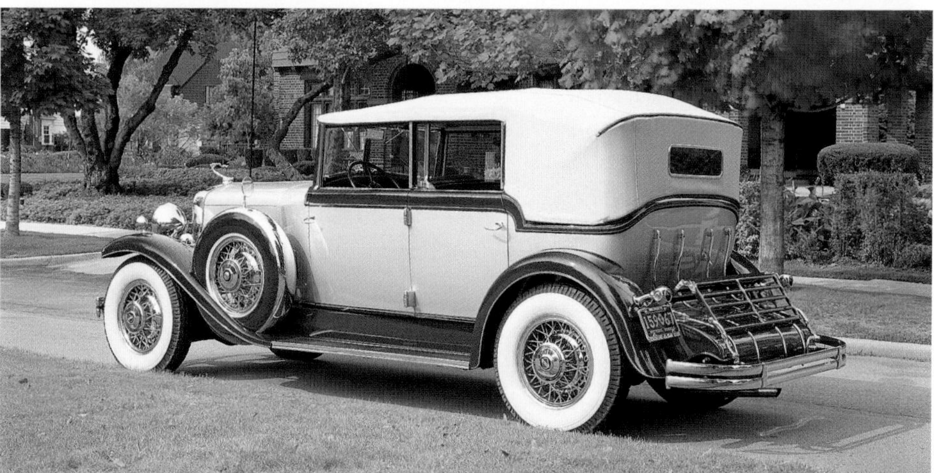

This 1930 LaSalle Fleetway four-door convertible is a rare sight, the body and style primarily seen on Cadillacs, not LaSalles. This car featured a two-piece "V" windshield and an interior roll-up divider window.

Mesh" was, of course, a major advance, enabling even the most novice driver to change gears smoothly and silently. Before full-scale production was realized, 10 variations of the Syncro-Mesh were tested in 25 different cars run over 1.5 million miles at the GM Proving Ground, indicative of Cadillac thoroughness. Other 1929 advancements included improved internal four-wheel brakes (again mechanical); safety glass; adjustable front seat; and that future darling of the stylist, chromium plating. The engine was re-bored to 3 1/4 inches, resulting in a larger displacement of 328 cubic inches and 16 additional horses.

The LaSalle lineup was reorganized so that all closed and convertible bodies were mounted on the larger 134-inch wheelbase while the original 125-inch chassis was reserved for the roadster and phaetons. Prices ranged from $2,345 for the two-passenger roadster to $2,875 for the four-passenger phaeton, with Fleetwoods up to a whopping $4,900. Production held steady at 22,961 units, which meant that during three model years the division had built nearly 50,000 editions of a brand-new, relatively expensive automobile, quite an achievement for even General Motors.

Yet despite that apparent success one has to question how much faith Cadillac had in its original concept. For scarcely three years after its introduction, LaSalle had moved away from the compact luxury car concept. With the 1930 models all LaSalles, from the two/four passenger roadster to the seven-passenger Imperial sedan, were mounted on the 134-inch chassis, nine inches longer than the 1927 series. Whereas in 1928 there had been a difference of 15 inches in wheelbases between LaSalle and the smallest Cadillac, there was now but six inches difference. True, the LaSalle's price range remained constant, meaning that the buyer was getting a bigger, more spacious car for his money,

Rounded lines were pronounced across the 1932 LaSalle lineup. Left: 1932 LaSalle 345 town sedan. Right: 1932 LaSalle 345-B victoria coupe.

but is this what he really wanted? Perhaps Cadillac felt compelled to up the wheelbase of the LaSalle as a result of competitive pressure. Many of LaSalle's competitors—the Packard 733, the Pierce-Arrow 133 Standard Eights, the Peerless and the Graham Custom Eights—all had models with wheelbases 134 inches or longer selling directly in LaSalle's price range. Once again, the traditionally American "bigger is better" philosophy triumphed.

Not that the 1930 LaSalle was a bad car. Mounted over the now-standard 134-inch chassis were new Fisher/Fleetwood bodies, styling being altered by making the radiator 2 1/2 inches higher than previously seen. The six-model Fleetwood line used names like "Fleetcliffe" and "Fleetshire" to designate the custom coachwork. On the mechanical side, bore was upped again to 3 5/16 inches, while the stroke remained the same, the result being a new displacement of 340 cubic inches. Horsepower was now 90. But with Cadillac's immense 452-cubic-inch V-16 receiving the acclaim of the motor press, LaSalle dropped out of the limelight it had enjoyed since its introduction. More importantly, production dropped sharply, only 14,995 of the 1930 Model 340 LaSalles being assembled. Wall Street had laid its famous egg and car buyers could sense the impending Depression. Luxury cars (of any size) were the first to feel the effects of the slackening economy.

Management's reaction to economic despair and falling production was a curious mixture of advancement and retreat. To further entice the remaining luxury-car buyers, a new 368 V-12 was brought cid out under the Cadillac nameplate as the LaSalle was simultaneously stripped of its separate identity. The 353-cubic-inch Cadillac V-8 was adopted as the LaSalle powerplant, and was to remain so through 1933. In an effort to promote greater interchangeability of parts among all Cadillac-produced cars, the LaSalle became, in every way possible, a mechanical twin of the Cadillac V-8. In addition, the wheelbase of most of the V-8 Cadillac models was reduced to 134 inches, so the two cars shared identical chassis as well. The main difference was the higher prices on the Cadillac (at least $500). Available in 12 body styles, the LaSalle's $2,195-$3,245 price range represented an average drop of $180. Detail improvements included single-bar bumpers and moving the battery under the front seat from its former position under the running board apron. Production fell again to 10,103 units, not as much as might have been expected. Still, on the registration lists more Cadillacs than LaSalles were sold to buyers, a situation that existed during 1930 as well.

During the 1932 and 1933 seasons, LaSalle offered an interesting car both aesthetically and mechanically. Body styling was new with more rounded lines and graceful "flying wing" fenders. Following the lead of Graham's famous "Blue Streak" model, LaSalle fenders were skirted in 1933. Also adopted that same year was a vee-d radiator grille and famous No-Draft ventilation as Fisher ended an era of drafty sedans and stuffy coupes. Once again management fiddled with the wheelbase, the 1932-33 line comprising four models on a 130-inch wheelbase and three additional styles on a larger 136-inch chassis.

Engineering changes included an improved Syncro-Mesh transmission with silent helical gears in all forward speeds, six-point engine suspension cushioned in rubber, and two-way hydraulic shocks adjustable by the driver. Offered also was that automotive fad of the early 1930s, free wheeling, combined with a vacuum-operated automatic clutch. The driver could disengage the clutch by pressing a conveniently located button below the clutch pedal, while letting up on the accelerator at the same time. Gear changing could then be accomplished and the clutch re-engaged by releasing the button or stepping on the gas. The clutch pedal could also be used in the regular manner if desired. During the two model years, horsepower was upped again to 115.

Downsized Competition

GM, as with most companies, was engaged in a continuous program of testing and evaluating competitive cars. This included the company's own cars as well. At the Proving Ground a 1933 Series 345-C LaSalle five-passenger sedan was duly tested, and the crew's opinions make interesting reading. While the No-Draft ventilation was found to be practical and efficient, the car's overall performance was rated below average. The crew was especially critical of the lack of rigidity in the front-end structure, which shook badly and even caused the spare wheels in the fender wells to vibrate. Chatter bumps caused shivers throughout the car. The report frankly stated that the problem might "hinder sales." A far greater hindrance of course was the Depression and production collapsed to 3,390 cars in 1932 and 3,381 in 1933. Consequently, LaSalle fell to 20th place or worse on the registration lists.

What was happening was obvious enough. The automotive market had changed completely since the LaSalle's introduction and luxury cars had become just that—a luxury that most people could not or would not afford. The LaSalle had been conceived in the expansive mood prevalent during the 1920s, along with such upper- and middle-priced makes as Viking, Marquette, DeSoto, Pontiac, Roosevelt. Of all of these aforementioned autos, only Pontiac and DeSoto had managed to get securely established despite the deepening Depression. Most of the new entries never had a chance.

Even at GM the Depression caused retrenchment. Chevrolet and Pontiac production lines were consolidated, as were Buick and Oldsmobile. Pontiac, Oldsmobile and Buick sales and dealer organizations were combined into a single division. The short-lived Viking and Marquette and even the venerable Oakland were unceremoniously dumped and there was talk of liquidating the entire prestigious but money-losing Cadillac-LaSalle operation. The GM management team, headed by Sloan, was a hard-headed, unsentimental bunch. Despite a promising start the LaSalle was clearly on its way out, at least in its familiar form.

LaSalle was the pace car for the 1934 Indianapolis 500. Speedway owner Eddie Rickenbacker (left) poses with driver Bill Rader.

The story is told (which may be apocryphal) that the decision had already been made to kill the LaSalle when Harley Earl persuaded management to look at what he had in mind for the nameplate for 1934. The officers came, they saw, and then gave their enthusiastic approval, ordering the car into production. However, it is unlikely that anyone at GM made the decision so lightly. Something was needed to pull Cadillac out of the red and put it back on a solid financial footing. It was decided to continue building cars under the Cadillac name for the remaining luxury market while also producing a cheaper car that would hopefully increase production to a profitable level. This car would bear the LaSalle name and the target price was $1,000 below the cheapest Cadillac.

This was achieved by clever use of off-the-shelf parts from other GM divisions. Replacing the expensive V-8 was an improved version from Oldsmobile's L-head straight eight block, introduced in 1932, with Lynite aluminum Lo-Ex pistons and a thermostatically controlled automatic choke. A counterweighted crankshaft was fitted with a vibration dampener at its front end. The five main bearings, connecting rods, wrist pins, camshaft bearings, and timing drive chain were all pressure lubricated. With a three-inch bore and a 4 1/4-inch stroke, the 240.3-cubic-inch engine developed 95 hp at 3700 rpm. Wheelbase was slashed to 119 inches, making the new series not only the smallest LaSalle ever but also the cheapest ($1,595-$1,695).

The most significant engineering innovation was the "Knee-Action" independent front suspension that was new to this country, although it had been used on European cars for some time. Chief supporter of the change from the solid front axle was Maurice Olley, although credit must also be given to Henry Crane, Ernest Seaholm (Cadillac chief engineer), Charles Kettering, Owen Nacker and a number of unheralded Cadillac and Buick engineers.

Olley came to Cadillac from Rolls-Royce in November 1930, concentrating his efforts on developing a better riding car. Early in 1932 a seven-passenger

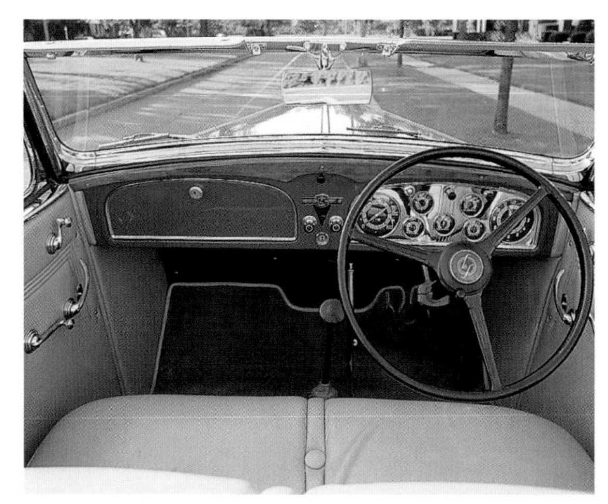

This right-drive 1934 LaSalle 350 convertible was shipped to Argentina. Available this model year were disappearing spare tire compartments.

limousine, nicknamed the "K-2 Rig," was constructed, which enabled the engineers to alter various aspects of a car's springing by movable weights. In this way they could test various "rides" and so found that a flat ride was highly desirable. Attempts were made to achieve this by using extremely soft front springs with a conventional front axle. But the result was shimmy and lack of stability, as the Proving Ground crew found when they tested the 1933 LaSalle.

With the support of Lawrence Fisher, two experimental cars were constructed at Cadillac at a cost of over a quarter of a million dollars. These cars had two different types of independent front suspension, one designed by French engineer André DuBonnet, who was collaborating with GM, the other one a "wishbone" type developed at Cadillac. Independent rear suspension was also tested, Olley feeling that the time had come to get rid of the conventional rear axle as well. After much development work the cars were ready for demonstration.

In March 1933, the members of the GM Technical Committee, including Sloan, Kettering and high division executives, assembled at the Cadillac Engineering Building to ride in the two experimental cars and a conventionally sprung Buick. The three cars were run to Monroe, Mich., and back, a distance of 70 miles.

However, within two miles of the Cadillac plant, the ride had sold itself. Olley hoped that Cadillac would be granted exclusive use of the new suspension for the first year, but the vastly improved ride was so impressive that every division wanted it. Even Chevrolet could not be turned down. So all GM cars had Knee-Action on their 1934 models, Chevrolet and Pontiac using the Dubonnet system and the others, including LaSalle, the wishbone type.

As used on the LaSalle, the system featured a kingpin carried on a vertical support arm, to the top and bottom of which were attached V-shaped or "wishbone" links, which were in turn hinged to the top and bottom of the frame. With the upper link the shock absorber was bolted to the top of the frame and acted as the frame hinge. The lower link was hinged to the frame with threaded bolts and bushings to take end thrust. The same kind of bearing hinge was also used at the upper and lower ends of the vertical knuckle support arm.

The wishbone links completely controlled wheel motion, permitting the wheel to move up and down in an almost vertical plane and also absorb side thrust and brake torque reaction. Coil springs were employed, since if a leaf spring had been used it would have had to be extremely long to give the required softness without overstressing the spring. To guard against bottoming with the softer coils, rubber bumpers were installed inside the coils. Alternately, overexpansion was prevented by placing another rubber bumper on the frame where the upper link might make contact if it swung down too far. Individual tie rods to the wheels were required to obtain proper steering geometry. Torsional stabilizer bars were used at the rear to help prevent side sway, resistance to which was lessened by the softer coil springs.

Eventually this wishbone type proved easier and cheaper to manufacture and more trouble-free, and was adopted by all General Motors cars. Actually, the Olley-designed independent front suspension is the basis of many of today's modern suspension systems.

The other important mechanical change was the adoption (finally) of hydraulic brakes. Hotchkiss drive was also adopted, replacing the torque-tube construction that characterized Cadillac products for the past six years.

To top off this new package, Harley Earl and the Art and Colour Section came through with another styling triumph equal to that achieved on the 1927 model. Body lines were completely new, modern and dramatic. All traces of the old "classic" styling vanished under Earl's supervision, replaced by smooth, clean, almost austere body planes. Even the spare tire disappeared, concealed in the fastback trunk, though fenderwell spares were available. The smoother look was relieved by such accents as porthole louvers on the hood sides and open, double-bar bumpers with telescoping spring mounts. Wire wheels were covered to resemble discs. Pontoon fenders and the streamlined bodies gave the car a much more substantial look which was to influence heavily all GM car lines during the 1930s. But the focal point of the new styling was a very narrow, vertical radiator grille. This slim-nosed look was to serve as LaSalle's trademark through the 1940 model.

By boldly striking out into a new design direction, LaSalle stood clearly above its competition, most of whom were still trying awkwardly to adjust to streamlining. The model line was reduced to just four body types—sedan, club sedan, coupe and convertible coupe—all by Fleetwood, with "unlimited" choice of color schemes.

With its new lower price the LaSalle moved into a different market entirely, competing with such cars as the Auburn V-12, Nash Ambassador 8, Reo-Royale 8, Buick Series 34-90 and Airflow Chrysler Imperial.

In 1937, a new, curved "egg-crate" grille was featured, as was a more streamlined top and new, elaborate hood ports with six narrow chrome strips, and three chrome chevrons on the leading edge of the front fenders. Above: 1937 LaSalle business coupe.

enabled Cadillac to produce and sell an encouraging 13,004 LaSalles, yet LaSalle still ranked behind the Zephyr (at 15,482) and far behind Packard's 120B (55,042). While a Proving Ground report on the Series 36-50 LaSalle stated it was a "very good appearing car with fair riding and good handling characteristics and considerable in-built quality," the public just wasn't responding with enough orders.

It became clear that the straight-eight LaSalle, however brilliantly styled, was failing to achieve the hoped-for production volume, so another try was made for 1937. A V-8 engine was returned to the car, this time borrowed from the 1936 Cadillac Series 60. This L-head V-8, which was to serve LaSalle to the end, had a 3 3/8-inch bore and a 41/2-inch stroke for a displacement of 322 cubic inches. Peak horsepower of 125 was developed at 3400 rpm and the compression ratio was 6.25 to 1. The increased power made possible a reduction in the axle ratios, so that pistons in the 1937 V-8 traveled only 2,100 feet during one driving mile compared with 2,360 feet in the former straight eight. Other mechanical advances included an improved engine-mounting system, a carburetor with two float bowls to avoid fuel starvation on sharp turns, oil-bath air cleaner, hypoid rear axle, and a new exhaust system with a single large muffler instead of the two smaller units used before. Oscillation rates of both rear springs and Knee-Action units at the front were changed to produce a softer ride at low speeds and a smoother ride at higher speeds. Roadability was improved by the use of a torsional stabilizer at the front and a Panhard-derived track bar at the rear. Waxed liner inserts between the leaves of the rear springs guaranteed permanent lubrication.

Wheelbase was lengthened to 124 inches and the frame was lowered and stiffened by the use of added X-members. Styling was typically GM—massive and well detailed. The bodies, with their narrow side windows, were shared with other upper-line GM cars. Five body types—two- and four-door sedans, coupe, convertible coupe and convertible sedan—were priced at an exceedingly low $995 to $1,485. The longer chassis gave increased passenger room and great attention was

Hard Decisions

The LaSalle was an impressive car and caused considerable stir among the more knowledgeable figures in the industry. One of these was Duesenberg president Harold Ames, who began planning a lower-priced Duesenberg using cheaper Auburn parts, in a frank imitation of the LaSalle concept. Ames got Gordon Buehrig to design a body for the experimental Duesie chassis and it was that car that ultimately emerged as the Cord 810. Strangely, Buehrig's concept was one Harley Earl had rejected during Buehrig's brief tenure at GM.

But the motoring public was unfortunately not as impressed. Perhaps the Depression was still too fresh in buyer's minds. At any rate, only 7,128 1934 LaSalles and 8,653 of the similar 1935 model were produced, which must have come as a tremendous disappointment to Cadillac officials. In the meantime Packard was introducing its "120" line, which not only undercut the LaSalle's price but also carried the immense prestige of the Packard name. Nearly 25,000 Packard 120s were produced and sold during 1935, cutting deeply into LaSalle's market.

Detail alterations on the 1935 LaSalles included lengthening the stroke on the straight eight to 4 3/8 inches, increasing displacement to 248 cubic inches. Horsepower was upped to 105 at 3600 rpm. Though styling remained virtually the same except for cheaper bumpers and a vee-d split windshield, Fisher's new all-steel "Turret Top" bodies were mounted on a wheelbase one inch longer. In response to Packard's bold thrust, prices were reduced so the cheapest LaSalle was now $1,255. This car was carried through 1936 substantially unchanged, except for minor styling changes and front doors hinged at the front for greater safety.

But Cadillac received some further bad news in the form of increased competition, this time from a new $1,275 Lincoln-Zephyr V-12. It seems as if every remaining luxury-car producer was getting the same idea at the same time. Another price cut to $1,175 base

given to more luxurious interiors.

The new model was heavily advertised as the lowest-priced LaSalle ever and completely rebuilt. It worked—the new styling, V-8 engine and advertising together with an improving economy, resulted in the production of 32,005 units, the highest production ever achieved for the marque. One result was that Cadillac divisional deliveries at retail reached a record high. Yet this placed LaSalle only slightly ahead of Zephyr and still far behind Packard's cheaper cars. The new model was carried into 1938 with minimal styling changes and mechanical improvements like a column-mounted gearshift and alligator hood. Assemblies declined to 15,501 in the face of an economic recession that killed Pierce-Arrow and fatally weakened Hubmobile and Graham.

LaSalle was caught in a difficult position, facing increased competition not only from the small Packards and Lincolns but also from a fast-rising Buick with its popular Century series. Time was running out on the junior Cadillac, but the LaSalle was given an additional two years to prove itself in the marketplace.

In common with other GM cars, new bodies were introduced on the 1939 LaSalles. One of the chief complaints on previous models was the narrow slit windows which cut driver visibility, so glass area was increased 27 percent on the new series. This change not only resulted in a lighter, more modern look but also contributed to safer driving. The trademark radiator grille was narrowed even further, becoming a slim column of brilliant chrome flanked by lower catwalk grilles. Apparently the sales people could not agree on a suitable chassis as the wheelbase was cut back to 120 inches, only to be increased three inches in the final year. Running boards disappeared except as options and in the convertible coupe, all four passengers sat inside under a common roof, eliminating the drafty, uncomfortable, dangerous—and sometimes delightful—rumble seat. On closed cars the customer could choose a "Sunshine Roof" option featuring a retractable metal panel over the driver's compartment. While this feature has more recently enjoyed a comeback, the original versions leaked so badly they were withdrawn after a short time. Redesigned pistons cut oil consumption and the rear suspension was altered. Assemblies increased to 23,028 for the model year.

LaSalle's final year was 1940, and let it be said that the marque went out with a flourish. Styling was refined with new sealed-beam headlights nestled into the fenders. Standard bodies included two- and four-door sedans, coupe, convertible coupe and convertible sedan, but the highlight of the line was the Special Sedan and Special Coupe. In mid-year a sleek convertible sedan and convertible coupe were added to the Special line. These cars, with their gently rounded "torpedo" forms and restrained detailing, were among the handsomest LaSalles ever built. Prices on the nine-body line began at $1,240 and went up to $1,895. Throat diameter of the dual downdraft Carter carburetor was increased one-eighth inch, resulting in 130 hp for the final V-8. Refinements in engine and chassis provided quieter operation and improved riding. Production in that final year totaled 24,133 as against 90,000 small Packards and 22,000 Zephyrs.

Time ran out for LaSalle by the 1941 model year. A lower-priced Cadillac Series 61 filled the gap. Opposite: 1940 LaSalle Series 52 convertible coupe.

There was a 1941 LaSalle program and Styling went ahead with its development, including full-size finished mockups. Photographs of these cars reveal that the 1941 model would have been merely a Cadillac with LaSalle grille and hood ensemble. Since the LaSalle had failed to garner the desired number of customers despite vigorous efforts to make it successful, division officials quietly discontinued the car at the end of 1940 after 14 years of honorable service.

For the 1941 season, a lower-priced Cadillac Series 61 was introduced at $1,345 to $1,535 to fill the gap left by LaSalle. It must have been the right move, because the division's production jumped from 37,162 to 66,130 in 1941, a new record. Cadillac became busy with handsome profits and the LaSalle was quickly forgotten.

All in all, over 205,000 LaSalles were built from 1927 through 1940, an average of only 15,000 a year. As a money-making venture the LaSalle was a failure and its production therefore came to an end. But why did it fail? After all, it had "everything"—distinctive good looks, solid engineering, and the backing of the world's largest automobile company. How could it lose?

The classic 1927-1933 line was doomed by the Depression. The market for smaller luxury cars collapsed along with the market for all luxury cars and LaSalle suffered with the rest. You couldn't sell $2,500 cars to people out of work and those who had jobs were more interested in $500 V-8 Fords. Although the 1934-1940 cars were excellent values in their price field, the LaSalle name actually hurt sales. The cars were Cadillacs in everything but name, but that was the key factor. Remember that both Packard and Lincoln marketed their cheaper cars under their own names, thus lending the prestige of the luxury cars to their medium-priced running mates. Despite Cadillac's strenuous efforts to promote the LaSalle nameplate the pubic generally preferred to buy Packard 120s and Lincoln-Zephyrs with their big-car names and status.

By 1941 Cadillac had finally realized what was happening and imitated their competitors by putting the Cadillac name on the division's cheapest car, something they probably should have done in 1934. When Cadillac's medium-priced car was named LaSalle, it was a commercial failure. When it was finally graced with the magical Cadillac name, the result was the greatest year in Cadillac history up to that time, proving once more that you can't beat the sales appeal of a well-known and well-respected marque.

"And Then the English Cars Came."

The G-Modified Revolution

Many think that the lightweight mid-engine race car is a recent development. But by 1955 a concept was created that would set the pattern for today's racers. It was refined through the late fifties, early- and mid-sixties into Can-Am cars and Formula One designs.

BY CARL GOODWIN

As sports and sports racing cars developed from the postwar period to the late sixties, the evolution was led not by the big-bore cars but by the second-to-smallest class, G-Modified, the 1100 class. G-Modified rapidly progressed from the frame-rail chassis of, essentially, the prewar era MGs, to the platform chassis of the Siata Spyder, to the tube frames of Cooper, Elva, Lotus and Lola; from front engine to rear engine.

The racing scene in America was probably the best illustration of this, with development of the Sports Car Club of America (SCCA) based upon European classes but with a far wider variety of cars than any European country. Initially, we had no American sports cars. That would be corrected by Briggs Cunningham and later Corvette and still later Shelby's Cobra, but in the early days American enthusiasts brought in the best cars from Italy, Germany, France and England. We had more money, more race courses, and the customs duty on an imported sports car was only 2 percent.

Both of our small-displacement classes – G-Mod and the 750cc H-Modified class – were initially dominated by Italian cars. The first of these were the Cisitalia coupes at Watkins Glen in 1949, and the Fiat 1100MMs in 1950. Then there were the little Siata Spyders. The prototype was driven by Otto Linton in 1951. Oddly enough, it was a tube-frame car weighing 150 pounds less than the production version with a platform chassis. These sweet-handling cars, resembling miniature Ferraris, were imported by Tony Pompeo. Some had a factory-installed Fiat 1100, for G-Modified, and some had no engine, intending them to be powered by the ubiquitous Crosley 750cc single-overhead-cam engine, for the H-M version.

The G-Mod Siata driven by John Bentley, the familiar no. 77 car, would have won the national championship in 1954 except for one thing: the 1100cc OSCA of Rees Makins. Luckily for everyone else, there were only a couple of these G-Mod twin-cam OSCAs in the country.

About that time, in 1954, a few of the cars made by Nardi were brought in. One of these was sold by Tony Pompeo to Frank Dominianni as a Giaur because it had been owned and modified by Giaur builder Berardo Taraschi.

"The Giaur was set up for a G-Modified Fiat 1100 engine," Dominianni said. "I decided to put a Crosley in it. The car originally had Fiat disc wheels but one of them came off at Watkins Glen. Tony Pompeo ordered some Borrani wire wheels for me, and bigger brakes. The car was great. It had a tube frame, aluminum body and, as I recall, weighed 940 pounds."

Other "Etceterini" cars in G-Mod and H-Mod included Stanguellini, Moretti (beautiful car but a little heavier than necessary), and the Fiat 1100-powered Abarth with dramatic "razor edge" bodywork by Boano. Stanguellini later built a very successful Formula Junior.

At the end of this evolution came the Bandini. It featured oval steel tubes welded upright, perhaps the first automotive application from aircraft practice, an innovation of Ilario Bandini. It was lighter than the Siata although it didn't handle quite as well, but it was faster on a road course. These cars were made in three sizes: baby bear, momma bear and papa bear, or 750, 1100 and 1400cc. Like most small Italian cars, they were imported by Pompeo. One of the 1100cc G-Mod Bandinis had good results in the hands of Cleveland driver Dick Gent but a 750cc version he also owned

Left: Dueling Siatas—The No. 91 H-M Siata Spyder of Chuck Stoddard drives around the No. 42 H-M Siata Spyder of Al Beasley. Both would go on to win multiple SCCA championships. Right: Dick Gent in his Cisitalia roadster at Akron in 1954.

was the national champion in H-Modified with Mel Sachs at the wheel.

One weakness the Italian G-Mod cars had was the engine, usually a Fiat 1100. George Jasberg was a racing mechanic at Momo's. He noted: "It was a three-main bearing engine and the stock cranks varied widely in quality. The ones for Stanguellini were okay, but many others were not. When Paul Ceresole drove his Cisitalia roadster in the '52 Vero Beach race, it broke a crankshaft. It broke at the edge of a throw and he brought the car to Momo's for repair."

In spite of shortcomings, the small-displacement Italian cars did set the standard for a time. In the book produced by Dino Bandini, Franco Verni, the shop boy at the Bandini works, recalled, "Many people tested Bandini cars. Mr. Chapman, Mr. Bracco and the other famous men tested. Then the Coopers ... and then the English cars came."

The English cars came indeed. Among the first in the United States were the Lotus Mk VI sports cars imported, of all things, by Pompeo, who knew an interesting car when he saw it. According to Jasberg, a Mk VI former owner, these were built between 1952 and 1955. "During 1955, there were some Mark 6s made with Mark 9 features, including de Dion rear ends, 11-inch Elektron brakes and Coventry-Climax engines," noted Jasberg, who owned one of the hybrid 6/9 cars. "The Mark 9 was made in 1955 only, and the Mark 11 from 1956 to 1958. They just made everything else except the Cooper Bobtail obsolete. The Series 1 used a split-beam front suspension just like the 8s and 9s did. The Le Mans model offered the 1100 FWA or the 1500 FWB engine. Beginning with the Series 2, the Formula II Mark 12-type suspension was used. It was a double-wishbone design." Soon Pompeo was bringing in Mk 9s and then Mk 11s, including one for Briggs Cunningham.

Concurrently, John and Charles Cooper had been running their open-wheel, single-seat Formula III cars in American events, through drivers like the great Paul Richards, Lex DuPont, George Alderman and others. The Bobtail T39 Cooper was developed out of the

Top: It's a rare spin for ace driver Tom Payne in the No. 184 Porsche Spyder as the No. 11 H-M Bandini of Chuck Hassan drives by during the 1957 Akron Airport sports car races. Above: The Italian interpretation of a small-displacement racing car is seen in the leading No. 27 Bandini and the No. 89 "Giaur" at Virginia International Raceway in 1958. Jim Eichenlaub is in the No. 27 car and No. 89 is Sandy McArthur's.

Left: Chuck Dietrich blasts through a corner at the 1957 Akron Airport sports car race in his Elva Mk I. Above right: Dietrich drives his Elva Mk I at Put-in-Bay in 1957. His entry is crumpled after running into an earthen berm. In the same race, Tom Hallock drives the new generation of sports cars, a Cooper Bobtail (below right).

Formula III chassis in 1955. It had a 65-pound frame. There were only two distributors in the United States: Leech Cracraft in Wheeling, W.V., and one on the West Coast. Cracraft drove the no. 55 single-seat Bobtail at Sebring in March 1956 and Ed Hugus drove no. 56. "It was a fine little car," Hugus said.

Cracraft finished 1st in class G, and 21st overall, ahead of Doc and Peg Wylie's Lotus 9, while the Hugus car DNF'd. Then in July, Hugus co-drove a Bobtail at Le Mans with John Bentley. "That was the first two-passenger Cooper," Hugus said. "I asked John Cooper how long it had taken to develop. He told me, 'Pops and I sat down at the pub one night and drew it up, and then we built it the next day.'

"The car was very good. We were leading our class until 7 or 8 o'clock Sunday morning when the right rear brake drum broke and I spun the car. I drove into the pits and John Cooper was jumping up and down on the pit wall. This is when you could only do maintenance at certain times. He told me to go around another three laps and come in for a repair. They did crimp the brake line though. When I came in again they replaced the drum and we finished the race on three wheel brakes."

It was one of the first cars to use Coventry Climax power, as Burdette Martin recalled: "I was at Cooper's in 1954 and John took me over to a shelf where he had the engine under a small tarp. 'This is the new Coventry Climax engine,' he told me. But I didn't think too much of it at the time." The advantage of this rear-engine configuration was not immediately apparent and the difference between a "Bobtail" and a Lotus Mk IX – in terms of speed – was the flip of a coin.

This Cooper did not gain a following in America because only a few were sent by the factory. As Chuck Dietrich noted, "The Cooper might have been more successful in racing if there'd been more Coopers. People would have developed the car and they'd have won more." To which Jess Wylie added, "There weren't a hell of a lot of them over here. Lance Reventlow raced one, and one of them finished ahead of me at Sebring when I had the Lotus 9."

M.R.J. Wylie, whom everyone called "Doc," had these lightweight English cars from 1955 to 1970. He had a doctorate in chemistry and was a vice president at Gulf Oil in Pittsburgh. "It started with the 500cc class," Wylie said. "They had to make them lighter and lighter so they adopted tube frames very early. John Cooper and Charles Cooper did. Then the others did it. I was driving a C-Type Jaguar until 1955. Then I bought the Le Mans car, a Lotus 9. It was a special car that Chapman had made ultra-light. It was an experimental car. You could see where tubes had been welded on and then cut off to reduce weight. It had Borrani alloy wire wheels and even the knock-off hubs had been machined lighter.

"It was a small, nimble, fast car, and it was the first Lotus to have disc brakes. At Sebring in '56 Fangio

Left: At the 1957 Glen Classic, Chuck Dietrich in the No. 107 Elva Mk II gets an enthusiastic checker. Right: A brand-new, unpainted Elva Mk II is seen at the Nassau Bahamas race in 1957. The cars had aluminum bodies at that point. Below: This Lotus 11 set the second-fastest time of the day at the 1957 Mt. Equinox hill climb, after the D-Type Jaguar of Harry Carter. Driving the Lotus was Major Warren Smith, a B-47 pilot from Omaha, Neb.

couldn't pass it in the corners – his Maserati couldn't corner and brake with the Lotus. It was that way for a long time with the small cars. That's how Moss and Lloyd won Sebring in the OSCA. Our Coventry-Climax engine only weighed 215 pounds. With SU carburetors it got 80 horsepower and with Webers 100 or 105. If you didn't break, you could win with it.

"I drove it from 1955 to '59 and then my wife took it over. Then I got the famous no. 58 Lotus 11 that won Le Mans in the 750 class. It was also very light. It was the first car to have the magnesium wobbly wheels. Colin put an 1100 engine in it. That was also a very successful car."

Longtime racer Chuck Dietrich had competed successfully in a supercharged MG-TC and a Harry Lester-built MG. In 1955 he placed 3rd in SCCA national points in the Lester. "Then I read an article in an English car magazine by John Bolton – it was on a car called an Elva," Dietrich said. "It sounded interesting, so I got in touch with Frank Nichols, the builder. It just so happened that Nichols had a car available."

Dietrich bought the Elva and began winning races almost immediately. This was the beginning of the front-engined era for the new wave of English cars. "Compared to the Lester and the Italian cars," Dietrich said, "they were much quicker. They cornered better, had better brakes and were totally different. They were superior cars. The early Elvas had special aluminum drum brakes, and they also had magnesium wheels."

Dietrich's first race in the Elva was at Watkins Glen in 1956. Then he drove at Put-in-Bay and the Akron Airport sports car races. "I did not do well that first race, but then I won every race after that," Dietrich said. Another early contest pitted the Mk I Elva against the Mk IX Lotus, at Brynfan Tyddyn. "I got into the lead very soon," Dietrich recalled. "The Elva was ideally suited to the course at Brynfan Tyddyn. I loved that course. The Lotus was a good, fast car that had done well in England, and Duncan Black was a good driver, but they fell behind."

Frank Nichols would update his cars almost every year, according to Dietrich, so the Mk II was introduced in 1957, the Mk III in 1958 and so on. The chronology of models, according to Elva factory records supplied by Chuck and Jane Dietrich, was: Mk I – 1956; Mk II and II B – 1957; Mk III – 1958; Mk IV – 1958 – 59; Elva DKW Formula Junior – 1959 – 60; Elva Mk V – 1959 – 60; Elva Formula Junior Series 2 rear engine – 1961; Elva Mk VI – 1961; Elva Formula Junior 300 – 1962; Elva Mk VII – 1963-65; Elva Porsche Mk VII & Mk VIIS – 1964; Elva Mk VIII – 1966.

For the most part, the G-Modified cars ended with the Mk VI, although a few Mk VII G-Mods were seen. Chuck Dietrich was very influential in introducing the English-style cars in America. As one of the leading drivers in the Midwest and East, he demonstrated how light cars with advanced suspensions could really go fast. He inspired other drivers to drive the new breed

Above: The most advanced of all the front-engined G-Modified cars was the Lola Mk I, seen here as the silver No. 78 at the Watkins Glen Grand Prix in 1960. Below: Dietrich's Bobsy in a fast sweeper. Dietrich won the SCCA national championship in 1963 in this Ford-powered machine with an aluminum tubular frame. Right: Another sign of the new wave of sports cars in G-Modified is this Lotus Mk VI driven by Bud Pell at Put-in-Bay in 1959. He's followed by Bo Miske in a Frazer-Nash.

of racing car and he generated interest not only in Elva but Lotus, Lola and Cooper as well.

In Europe, Lotus activity was increasing, as George Jasberg noted: "There were five Lotus 11s at Le Mans in 1957. One of them had a special 750cc Climax engine. Driven by McKay Frazer and Jay Chamberlain, it placed 1st in Class and 11th overall, taking the Index of Performance away from the French. Also in '57, at Sebring, Colin Chapman and Joe Shepperd drove to a 1st in class and 11th overall. In 1958, the Series 2 Elevens came out, with double-wishbone front suspension. They had a remarkable success at the '58 Sebring, with three of them in the top 10, all in Class G. The 4th place by Weiss and Tallaksen was their highest overall finish in a major race. In 1959, the top 1100 car at Sebring was an Elva driven by Frank Baptista, Art Tweedale and Chuck Wallace. That year the Lotus Type 17 was introduced. It used the Coventry FWA or FWM but was made only one year."

In 1960, Doc Wylie bought a drum-brake Lola. None of the new disc-brake cars were available and he bought this one used in England. "The drum brakes were large and very good," Wylie said. "The first time we raced, at the Road America 500 enduro, we won our class. We raced with the same oil and water in the engine as it had in England. By 1962 I knew Eric Broadley pretty well and I bought a new Lola with disc brakes. The Lola was a good car – nothing could beat it."

Longtime SCCA and FIA official Burdette Martin drove a Lola Mk 1 in 1960. "After you drove a Lola there was nothing else like it," Martin said. "A good G-Modified car could not get under 3 minutes at Road America but the Lola could be 5 seconds under that. It was unbeatable until the Lotus 23 came along."

Martin recalled the time Lola designer Eric Broadley came to the United States and drove in a race at Smartt Field, just outside of St. Louis, in 1959. "It was the last year that Broadley ever drove," Martin said. "Eric was a good bit faster than I was but then he spun and I got

Top: The G and F-Modified class heads into turn one at the 1963 Glen Classic. An example of the evolution of earlier G-Modified technology was Dietrich's E-Modified Elva-BMW, seen here in 1964 (above right) and in front of the "Scuderia Tin Can" transporter at the 1964 USRRC, Laguna Seca.

past. I thought, 'Hah – I beat him.' There were only two laps left in the race but in those two laps he caught and passed me."

The Lola Mk 1 was the last fast front-engined car in G-Mod. Already, Cooper had moved up the displacement ladder from the 1100cc Bobtail, with the Mark I Monaco 21⁄2-liter sports car in 1959. This was followed by the Lotus 19 Monte Carlo, also 21⁄2 liter Coventry-Climax-powered. By 1961, a Monaco (Roger Ward's) would have an alloy Buick V8 installed by Bob McKee. Unfortunately, it DNf'd in major races.

Another step for Cooper, into larger-displacement models, was not works-built, but put together by an American racing patron, Mrs. Henry Clark Bowden. Her mechanics built what many believed was an ordinary Bobtail for Paul Richards to drive. George Alderman recalls that it was built in the late fifties or early sixties. As Lex duPont notes, it was actually a Formula II Cooper with sports bodywork. At the time, Formula II was the de facto Grand Prix car as Formula 1 was not accepted by the teams.

"It was originally a Coventry-Climax-powered Cooper," duPont said, "and I have no idea who put the Bobtail body on it. The engine, as Paul and my brother drove it, was a 1600 four-cam Porsche. After development it was 160 horsepower. Paul Richards won the race at Walterboro, N.C., against several Ferraris. Of course it didn't hurt that it was a wickedly hot day and the Ferraris were overheating."

Chuck Dietrich drove Elvas up until the early '60s when Gerry Mong asked him to test a new car. Mong, in Medina, Ohio – just outside Cleveland – constructed a G-Modified car with an aluminum tube frame. It was a beautiful machine and the workmanship, especially the aluminum welding, was outstanding. It was developed in 1961 and announced in 1962, the same year that the Lotus 23 was introduced.

"At that point, independent suspension and rear engines were the thing to do in a race car," Mong said. "I had previously built a special pattern after a Porsche 550, with a large-diameter perimeter frame, VW engine turned around, upside-down transmission and an aluminum body. Then I made a pair of identical hobby cars for two brothers, Kaye and Alan Hier. Their mother was there and she said, 'Oh, they look like the Bobsy twins.' I never liked the name, but it stuck. By the time the cars became popular, it was too late to change."

Suzy Dietrich recalled that Kaye Hier had his car at Cumberland, Md., and Mong asked if Chuck could take the car out for a couple of laps. He took the car out and

Clockwise from top left: In turn one at Thompson Raceway, 1962, Dave Fenton's Elva Mk VI battles a Lotus 23 copy called the Brama; Reed Andrews' No. 31 G-Mod Elva Mk VI sets up a pass on the No. 51 C-Type Jaguar of Art Seyler in an early-sixties race at Nelson Ledges in Ohio; a C-Modified Cooper Chevy at Meadowdale in 1964; the mighty Elva, driven by Andrews, leads the pack at Road America (Elkhart Lake, Wis.) June Sprints in 1966.

quickly put down some terrific lap times. Mong offered Dietrich a ride for the season, which resulted in a G-Modified National Championship for Bobsy in 1963.

"The one that Chuck Dietrich drove was the SR2," Kaye Hier said, "a short-nose version of the SR3. We campaigned it with him. He drove around a few of its deficiencies, including a suspension that was way too soft. The car weighed between seven and eight hundred pounds and it might have been a little too light to warm up the tires and get the handling right. "

The Bobsy had a Ford engine similar to those used in the Formula Juniors. The Merlyn was not as fast, according to Dietrich, and the Bourgeault that came later was a California special.

When the Lotus 23 debuted, it was initially powered by a 997cc version of the Ford 105E engine. English writer John Blunsden described it as "a wide Lotus 22 Formula Junior – the closest thing to a Lotus 22 Junior that is possible to make, the car will carry a scaled-down and smoothed-out Appendix C body." It made a dramatic debut in the hands of Jim Clark at the 1,000-km Nürburgring race in 1962, a 900-pound car powered by a 1500cc Lotus-Ford twin-cam engine. Clark was leading the Porsche and Ferrari entries by two minutes until he was overcome by fumes from a broken exhaust and crashed. Peter Sachs won an SCCA national title in the Lotus 23 in 1963, in class F-M; after which Jim Baker of Atlanta won the G-M title in a 23 in 1965 and Charlie Gibson's Lotus won it again in 1967.

Then Merlyn built a sports racing car for the G-Mod and F-Mod classes in North America, a year after the Lotus 23 was introduced. Called the Mark 6, it was derived from the mid-engined Merlyn Mark 5 Formula Junior. The G-Mod car weighed 719 pounds and had a 123hp Cosworth Mk 17 engine. In America, three distributors promoted the car through racing: Bill Bradley's Black Hawk Automotive in Detroit, Sterling Auto in Los Angeles and Charlie Barnes in Dallas. Bradley won the F-Modified Central Division title in 1963 and Barnes won G-Modified at the Road Race of Champions in 1964.

The evolution continues. Left to right: A Formula One car in 1964, Jim Clark's Lotus at the Watkins Glen Grand Prix—note that the top front A-arms are gusseted so the springs can be mounted out of the airstream; by 1971, the mid-engine open-wheel cars were starting to sprout wings, with even wider tires, as seen on this Ferrari at Ontario Motor Speedway in '71; the beautiful McLaren 4B is not conceptually different from the Cooper Bobtail, as seen here with the car in which Dietrich won the SCCA National Formula B Championship in 1967.

British Invasion

By now, the English cars had edged out the heavier, less advanced Italian makes, none of which really upgraded their cars. Of the British "big four" – Cooper, Lola, Lotus, Elva – it is interesting that all but Elva had a Formula One car. The smaller constructors like Merlyn, Alexis and Gemini would continue in FJ and the soon-to-be Formula Ford, while Brabham would evolve from Cooper, McLaren would evolve from Elva, and builders like March and Chevron would later appear on the scene.

And what of the influence of Porsche in advancing the new technology? After all, they had engines in the back, too. But they were a little slow to embrace the small-diameter tube frame, so they did not benefit from the weight savings possible. They used 3-inch tubes while Elva used 1-inch tubes. As longtime Elva driver Chuck Dietrich noted, "They were just too heavy. They were about 1,300 pounds and we were about 800." Their suspension systems were different from those of the English cars. Their ride height was greater. Their four-cam powerplant was 125 pounds heavier than the pushrod engine of the production cars. It was not uncommon for an 1100cc Elva to beat a 1600cc Porsche Spyder.

As early as April 1962, Briggs Cunningham debuted a Cooper Monaco with a Reventlow aluminum Buick in the back. This one finished races and set records at Watkins Glen. Roger Penske and Roy Gaine then took the Cooper concept to its next level, with the center-seat sports racing Zerex Special, based on a repaired, re-powered (2.7) and re-skinned Cooper Formula One car that Walt Hansgen had wrecked practicing for the 1961 Watkins Glen GP. Penske bought it from Briggs

Cunningham for $1,500. It won the Riverside and Laguna Seca grands prix in fall 1962. In 1963, Carroll Shelby put a 289 Ford in a Cooper Monaco for Bob Holbert to race at Laguna Seca, the same year that Jim Clark's Lotus Formula One car was on the grid in South Africa with a weight of 990 pounds.

After that the British model, led by innovations at the Cooper works, expanded in America to the larger-displacement sports racing classes with the Cooper Monaco, reaching its zenith with the Can-Am class beginning in 1966: big American V8s in lightweight English chassis, such as Cooper-Fords, Cooper-Chevys, Lolas, McLarens and Chaparrals. These cars were faster than the Formula One machines, and the Can-Am Series was immensely popular for many years. Essentially the same chassis in an open-wheel single-seater with a different engine is an F1 or Indy car.

Today, all pure racing cars are based on the mid-engined G-Modified cars of the mid-fifties. To date, the evolution is complete.

SANDS OF TIME

The World's Battleground of Speed

Scarce three miles from the Daytona International Speedway, on the margin of the Atlantic Ocean, is a wide shore of packed sand where, at the beginning of the last century, men and machines of many countries won wide renown with their exploits of speed. This is the story of that beach on which speed records were set and lives were lost, as told by the late Fred Booth, veteran editor and reporter for the **Daytona Beach News-Journal**. *At the time Booth compiled his eyewitness accounts for AQ in the early 1960s, he was the only newsman living to have covered all the record trials on the beach from 1927 through 1935.*

BY FRED BOOTH

AN ALL BRITISH TRIUMPH
207 Miles per Hour!
THE HIGHEST SPEED EVER ATTAINED ON LAND
On March 29th 1927, Major H. O. D. Segrave, driving a Sunbeam Car lubricated with Wakefield Castrol, broke World's Records for 1 Kilometre, 5 Kilometres and 1 Mile, reaching a speed of over 207 m.p.h. one way of the course.
SUNBEAM
Using
WAKEFIELD
Castrol
MOTOR OIL

Left: "Wild Bob" Burman poses in a Buick for a race against an airplane at a Daytona Beach "speed festival" in 1910. Above: Sir Henry Segrave.

The hey day of the speed trials on Daytona and Ormond beaches was a time when automobiles had gained such power and capacity of speed that there were few roads, if any, on which they could be driven safely at full throttle. Indeed there weren't many roads where cars could be driven in safety at any speed.

Waiting for the drivers and machines of those days was that piece of natural magic in Florida – the wide, sandy beach, firm and smooth, reaching all the way from Ormond to Daytona Beach and on south some 15 miles to Ponce de Leon Inlet. From time immemorial this beach had been there, but not the automobile. There was rejoicing, a great stir in many lands where the internal power buggy had gained favor, when word of the old, new-found track got abroad. New history began to take shape. The miraculous beach, without changing, began to play a part in one of the profound changes of history. It was a revolution of men and machinery that thrilled the thoughtless and turned thoughtful men to thinking and planning.

When you study the engineering of the International Speedway at Daytona Beach, you are looking at something that had begun to take shape in the secret processes of men's minds when the automobile was invented, and when somebody first beheld that broad sandy beach on Florida's East Coast and comprehended its immense potential in the running and testing of cars. Thus when we cheer the drivers as they race at the speedway and observe another anniversary of speed in Daytona Beach, we celebrate ancient history. The gas and steam-driven cars that coughed and puffed up and down the great sand speedway more than a century ago are museum pieces now, prized for their comparative antiquity and the quaintness of their looks, prized too for what they mean as symbols of a new epoch in modes and standards of travel.

Great Men of Another Day

All the great men who figured in those early days of motorcar testing and competition on the beach – designers and drivers – are dead. So, too, are these men who performed with distinction in the revival of world's record trials here beginning in 1927 – Henry Segrave, Malcolm Campbell, Ray Keech, Frank Lockhart, Lee Bible.

In this story you may find much that is stirring, much that is saddening – all of it a significant part of the history of our time. It is significant for two reasons. The speed trials weren't mere spectacles, Roman holidays staged to draw crowds. They were sponsored by enterprising and imaginative manufacturers to improve the speed and general behavior of cars, their durability, their dependability under stress.

Glory or death, sometimes both, came to the drivers. Better cars came to all of us by their daring.

There was an even deeper meaning, of greater historic import. The super-powerful motors sent to the beach speedway by their British makers were designed for airplane service. The world's record speed trials were ground tests out of which came some of the technical factors in the creation of swifter and more powerful planes – the planes that went aloft bearing the hopes and prayers of all freedom-loving people at the outbreak of World War II.

Those British planes that grappled with the forces of frightfulness over the English Channel, and England itself, and the Continent – the thunder of their great motors triumphantly echoed what we had heard a few years earlier on the world's Battleground of Speed.

Came An Irishman

On a sunshiny day in the winter of 1927, a small crowd gathered expectantly in front of the Clarendon Hotel (later called the Daytona Plaza). They were in a tizzy of glad excitement. They were waiting for the arrival of a man by the name of Henry O'Neill DeHane Segrave, an Irish-born Britisher.

Segrave was a famed automobile racer. He had won laurels on the great Brooklands track and on the dangerous road courses of the Continent and Ireland. Now he was coming to Daytona Beach, bringing with him a huge supercar with the avowed aim of shooting at a new world's land speed record on the ocean speedway. His target was the almost undreamed-of figure of 200 mph.

On this day word had come that he had arrived in Jacksonville and was driving down, but not of course in his world's record challenger. So here waiting to welcome him was a reception committee headed by Mayor Ed Armstrong. There were other city officials and chamber of commerce figures. Among them was Cassie B. Wingate, automobile dealer who used to drive souped-up cars in barrel races on the beach. Two eager members of the committee were Jack Reed, automobile dealer who had enthusiastically supported local automobile races, and Fred B. Nordman, owner of Number 9 Plantation, who was to become a genial friend and host to British and American actors in the speed trial revival. There were newspapermen, photographers – among them Dick LeSesne and Bill Coursen, later the city commissioner – plain citizens, automobile racing fans, mechanics and a sprinkling of boys.

A fleet yellow sports tourist car hove into view on North Atlantic. It swept to a stop in front of the hotel and a red-headed young man with pink cheeks and flashing blue eyes stepped out. Grinning pleasantly he said, "I'm Major Segrave." The mayor shook hands with him, introduced him all around, and solemnly promised the city's full cooperation in the young Irishman's attack on the world's record.

Segrave said his supercar, a two-engined Sunbeam that had been dubbed the "Mystery S" in England, was being shipped down in an express car. It would be here in a few days and would have to be towed to its oceanfront garage. Its speed and power were too much for street driving.

Segrave and his sizable staff were quartered in the Clarendon. A garage with tool shop was made ready across the avenue for his record challenger.

Thus began a revival of the speed trials on the beautiful ocean beach, which Associated Press writer Alan J. Gould some years later called "The World's Battleground of Speed." The Segrave revival came after a seven-year recess of record trials and races that had given the ocean shore international renown in the pioneer days of automobile design and competition.

Segrave took his giant 1927 Sunbeam 1000 to Daytona Beach to challenge Malcolm Campbell's record. The Sunbeam's power unit consisted of two V-12, 435hp, 48-valve Matabele aero-engines. In 1928, Ray Keech drove the White Triplex (far right) to 207.55 mph.

The Early Days

In the winter of 1903, the pioneering giants of the newborn automobile industry brought cars of their own design and manufacture to the beach to vie with each other for new speed records.

Alexander Winton brought his "Bullet." Ransom E. Olds, who later became a winter resident of Daytona Beach, brought one of his first Oldsmobiles. They stayed at the Ormond Beach Hotel and tracked the sand speedway from one end to the other with the wheels of their chugging, stinking vehicles. But they had a good time and won fame for their cars. Winton that year drove his "Bullet" a mile in 52.20 seconds – at the rate of 68 mph.

A year later a wealthy sportsman driver, William K. Vanderbilt, came bringing with him a foreign car, the

German Mercedes. Vanderbilt drove his beautifully designed car a mile in 39 seconds flat – a fraction above 92 mph. He drive it five miles around hairpin turns, marked out with barrels, in three minutes, 31 and one-fifth seconds – a speed of more than 85 mph.

The German car's performance carried the name of Daytona Beach to every country on the Continent, to the British Isles and even more distant places. The world was becoming speed conscious.

The next decade saw many of the world's best cars, most daring drivers and some of the smartest pioneer makers gathering on the wide beach winter after winter, jamming throttles wide open in the tense battle for more speed and learning ever more about what made automobiles tick. Daytona Beach had become the world's prime testing ground for experiments in design and construction. During those golden winters came many of the early heroes of speed, bringing with them new and mighty cars, their performance making news in all the capitals of the world. Their names held a big place then in the "Who's Who" of automobile making and racing: Arthur MacDonald with a Napier; H.L. Bowden and E.R. Thomas with their Mercedes; Paul Sartori with his Italian Fiat; H.W. Fletcher with a De Dietrich; designer Louis Chevrolet (guess the name of his car); F.E. Stanley and sewing machine tycoon Rollin H. White with their steam-powered cars; Barney Oldfield chewing his cigar butt and driving his German Blitzen Benz a mile in 27 and one-third seconds – a fraction over 131 mph.

One winter – in 1905 – there were 42 entrants in a program of speed trials and racing that ranged all the way from a kilometer to 100 miles. The local automobile club was a notable organization involved.

Speed's ascendancy over time leaped higher in 1906, again at the Ormond-Daytona Beach meet centering at Hotel Ormond, when Fred Marriott of Waltham, Mass., drove his Stanley Steamer a mile in 28.20 seconds, a speed of 127.65 mph, and Demogeot sent his Darracq over a two-mile stretch at a speed of 122.44 mph.

Here at least two winters was seen a tall, rawboned young man from Detroit who had designed and built a new car with the idea of bringing the cost down so thousands of persons could own one – not just wealthy sportsmen and businessmen; his name: Henry Ford. He was plagued with hard luck and the not-so-polite scorn of many of his contemporaries. Once a broken crankshaft balked him; another time it was a bent axle. There's a story that he lived in a tent on the beach and sometimes didn't have the price of a can of gasoline. In those days many in the auto game spoke of Henry Ford as just a rustic mechanic with hard oil on his thumb trying to horn into a game much too big for him.

Other elite of booming Gasoline Alley was here:

Top left: Keech in the White Triplex. Bottom Left: Malcolm Campbell and the Blue Bird in 1928. Above: Campbell, fifth from left, with engineers and the chassis of the latest Blue Bird construction.

Glenn H. Curtis with a motorcycle; "Wild" Bob Burman, driving a Fiat; David L. Bruce-Brown, wealthy Yale undergraduate who played hooky to drive in a 125-mile race for amateurs; Ralph DePalma, ace of the tracks; such famed foreign drivers as Italy's Lancia and Cedrino, France's Hemery and Renault.

Among the distinguished visitors in 1905 were the Duke of Manchester and Sir Walter DeWar.

It was in 1910 that Oldfield drove his Blitzen Benz 131 mph. A year later Burman in a Benz shoved it up to 141-plus. An eight-year recess in high-record driving followed. The annual 500-mile race on the brick-paved oval at Indianapolis had become the new magnet of high-speed competition. Other tracks had sprung up all over the country.

Then, in 1919, DePalma brought an American Packard to the beach and drive it a mile in 24.02 seconds – 149-plus mph. A year later, Tommy Milton, seasoned and brilliant track racer, came here with his American Duesenberg and drove a mile in 23.07 seconds. That was a notch above 156 mph. Years later, telling Henry Segrave and some of us newsmen about that feat, Milton said:

"I started rolling far north of the Clarendon and had my foot all the way down when I approached the Main Street Pier. Then, no more than a quarter of a mile ahead, I saw a long, lean man in a wide black hat and a chin whisker start backing a Model T Ford across the beach, right across my path.

"I couldn't slow down. I couldn't swerve from the course. I could only grit my teeth and hold on. The Model T got out of the way just in time. I heard something go 'ting' as I went by – I reckon it must have been my rear fender kissing his front one. I wonder if that man ever saw me."

After that came a seven-year recess on the beach, except for occasional hairpin-turn races for dirt track drivers and souped-up stockcars. Tracks and road courses and other beaches had captured the big names of speed – until the red-haired Irishman came with his "Mystery S."

Above: A gathering of the world's fastest men in 1928, left to right: Ray Keech, Frank Lockhart and Malcolm Campbell. Keech set the land speed record at that year's meeting. A year earlier, Lockhart hit the surf and would have likely drowned in his Stutz Blackhawk if not for the bravado of bystanders and fellow drivers.

Intellect and Daring

Segrave's decision to attack the world's land speed record at Daytona Beach came as a surprise to local officials. Even the American Automobile Association's national office at Washington knew nothing of his plans until they were reported in a news story from London.

Segrave showed in that first-published report of his plans that he knew more about the seashore at Daytona Beach than most Daytonans, more than AAA racing officials. He had learned the facts by skilled research.

On the basis of the knowledge thus gained, he had directed the secret design of the huge Sunbeam. It was made to fit the ocean speedway. He had completed the big car and had it ready to roll before announcing what he meant to do with it.

He knew at that time there had not been found any other strip of earth that could hold a car traveling at 200 mph. Segrave had designed and built the Sunbeam for that speed, on this particular strip of vacuum-packed sand. (It was years later that Bonneville Salt Flats in Utah was discovered, tested and proved to be a faster course than the ocean speedway.)

As with other speed seekers, Campbell (top) and Lockhart (above) designed and built their own land-speed crafts. They were truly one with their machines.

Buoyed with his facts and the engineering skill that had gone into the Sunbeam, Segrave came, confident but keyed up. In those days to talk of shooting at 200 mph took your breath away.

There was much talk in the hotel lobby – of gears, tires and tire expansion at superspeed, of wind resistance and streamlining (a new subject those days), of wind tunnels to test the effect of air resistance and methods of offsetting it. Segrave was a pioneer in scientific streamlining and in the use of a wind tunnel for experimentation with design in connection with wider research and calculation. His Sunbeam was one of the first streamlined jobs.

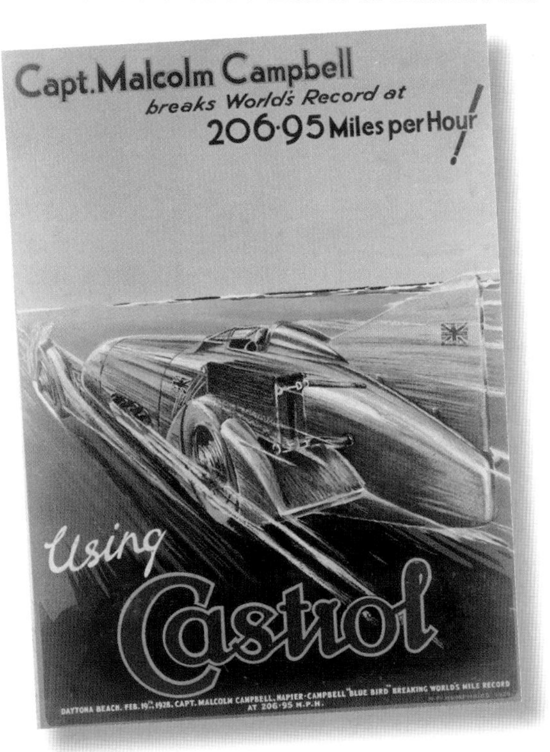

Segrave was a ready and brainy talker about automotive engineering and high-speed control, but not

Segrave with his Golden Arrow in 1929. Following his record-breaking success with the 1000hp Sunbeam, Segrave announced a new attempt in this all-new car. The Golden Arrow was designed by J.S. Irving and used a Napier Lion aero-engine of the Special 930hp Schneider Trophy type. The 12 cylinders were in a W formation.

about danger or about himself. He was no grandstander. He was fond of talking of international affairs, too, and amazingly well informed. We learned why. He had been an attaché of the British Embassy in Washington. He was a member of the British Overseas Club, a strong and outspoken advocate of Anglo-American friendship. In no time at all he had become immensely popular. Newspapermen liked him because he never broke a promise, never dodged a fair question, was never late to an appointment. He was liked for his graciousness, his lively sense of humor. His crew of mechanics and technicians worshipped him. No wonder. This Irish aristocrat – his father was a baronet – had a deep respect for all men regardless of position.

By the time the Mystery Sunbeam was ready to be unloaded at the railroad siding the town had worked itself into a fever of enthusiasm for this Briton and his mission of speed. A small multitude stood by while the huge red "Mystery S" was rolled out of its boxcar and tenderly unloaded, and while its massive wheels were put on. The multitude became a parade – a big one – when the car was towed through the streets and across the river to the garage for adjustments and tuning. Officials, businessmen, sedate matrons, speed fans, boys and girls followed along like kids tagging after a circus parade.

Meanwhile elaborate preparations had been started to make the beach course as safe as possible for the Briton's great adventure. A speed trials committee was formed and tasks were assigned to competent persons. The National Guard Company was readied to help police the course. Colored flags on short staffs were obtained, to be stuck at regular intervals along the speedway on the days of the trials, to make the driving safer. Meanwhile, officials of the AAA came and perfected arrangements to judge and time Segrave's attack on the world's record.

The record then stood at 174 mph. It had been set earlier that year at Pendine Sands in Wales by another Briton, Malcolm Campbell. That performance and the conditions overcome by Campbell had convinced Segrave the Welsh beach was no place for his big Sunbeam.

One of the AAA officials was Odis Porter, middle-aged, bullet-headed, jolly, who had invented an electric timing device with a trap wire to be stretched at each end of the measured mile. The device featured an electric clock, running tape and a printing device that would record elapsed time to one one-hundredth of a second.

Segrave was deeply touched by the elaborate preparations to safeguard his life and help him crack the record. He told us he had been warned in England that attempts would be made to sabotage his car – anything to prevent him from setting a new record.

"When I get back home," he said, "I shall tell all England what beastly lies were told me about you Americans, what good sportsmen and helpful friends you have been. It's more important, I think, for me to go back and tell that than it is for me to go riding at 200 miles an hour. Of course," he added, grinning, "I knew they were all lies or I shouldn't have come at all."

Segrave went into training for his supreme test, which he knew would come after a Northeast wind had ironed the beach out smooth and hard. No cigarettes. Early to bed, up early for work on the Sunbeam. Quiet talks in the early evenings with his friends, but not about racing.

Late in March a Northeast breeze sprang up. The word went out for everybody to get ready. Segrave looked at the tide table and set the time for the start of his first run. It would be early in the morning.

Preparation, Prayers and Cheers

This was the day. The morning dawned clear and cool. The tide was ebbing against the Northeaster's sustained drive. A check of the beach at low tide the night before found it already in prime shape. It would be even better this day.

So, early in the morning the siren in the Mainland Fire Station let loose with a long-drawn scream. That was the agreed signal. It brought out the National Guard, the police, the city engineers and electricians, the AAA officials with their electric timing device and their record sheets. All these men, hundreds of them, converged on the beach. The approaches were closed and guards were posted. The 13-mile course, from the Ocean Pier down to the Inlet, was staked out with colored flags.

Down at the south end of the measured mile the AAA officials set up shop on a row of tables on the upper margin of the beach, in the dry windblown sand. The timing trap wires were laid out, the electric voltmeters and the timing device were tested.

Coolly, the trials officials went about the routine of getting ready while we news reporters, new to this business, fiddled with our pencils and peered up the beach, craning our necks for the first glimpse of the Sunbeam and its driver.

The fire station's wailing cry had reached others besides the speedway crews. Everybody had heard it. Everybody knew what it meant – and everybody, nearly, headed for the beach. They came in big cars and little ones, old ones and new. They came on bicycles and on foot. A few rode horses. They streamed across the bridges and along the streets leading to the beach. Women trudged, their skirts flapping in the smart wind, pushing perambulators. Boys came running and whooping, forgetful of the school hour not far off.

Segrave was presented with a replica of the Golden Arrow, in which he set a new land speed record of 231.44 mph in 1929 (below).

Within the hour a motley multitude peopled the dunes. From near the pier, along the length of the beach clear to the Inlet they stood or sat. Thousands of men, women and children, quiet, intent, waiting. America's worship of speed was having its day.

Then came Segrave with his Sunbeam. We could see it far up the beach in the brilliant sunlight. They were towing it down to the timing stand, carefully, tenderly, as trainers and stable boys lead a tender-bitted thoroughbred to the starting post. A car and motorcycle led the way. Two police motorcyclists hugged the great monster's red flanks. Two others brought up the rear.

Cheers from the dunes greeted the slow cavalcade – feeble cries buffeted and muffled by the wind and the pounding surf. You could imagine there were some prayers among those childlike cries. Was there anybody there who didn't know the young man from across the ocean would be riding against death as well as time?

At the timing stand, checking over the final details before starting his first run, Segrave suddenly broke training. First he turned to me with his boyish grin and asked for a cigarette. Then others. For 15 minutes, while waiting for the official word to start, Segrave chain-smoked, accepting cigarettes from anyone because he had brought none along. We understood; the thoroughbred was champing the bit.

Then the word came, and soon the day's trials were over. First the Sunbeam was towed to the south end and Segrave drove it north. Then it was turned around and Segrave drove it south. You saw it looming up in the distance, then it swooshed by and was gone out of sight. In the cockpit between the great fore and aft engines you could glimpse the young driver's bright face and white helmet.

I was surprised it didn't make more noise. I had expected it to come by thundering and shooting lightning from its tail. It made a humming sound like a huge top.

The runs over with, Segrave came back to the timing stand to see if he had made the desired goal: 200 mph. Then came the anticlimax, the crushing disappointment. The Sunbeam had fallen far short. Something had gone wrong. Two bright red spots glowed in Segrave's cheeks. He was suffering great anguish of mind, anyone could see it. But he spoke quietly to his engineer and mechanics, and they began checking over the big car.

It didn't take them long to learn why the Sunbeam had failed in its first test. On each side of the body, opposite the front of the rear motor, was a shutter that could be opened at an angle to admit a free flow of air to the rear engine. These shutters had been closed to improve the streamlining. The result: The rear engine had been starved for air in that first run. The forward engine had done nearly all the work.

Greatly cheered, Segrave announced he would come out again the next day and make another try. He did, and within minutes after that bright face and white helmet had flashed by the timing stand twice, the word had gone out to all the world that a young Briton name Segrave had driven an automobile at the amazing speed of 203 mph.

Segrave went back to England singing the praises of his American friends and the great speedway. He knew and we knew the Sunbeam's performance had revived the world's record trials on the white quartz sand at Daytona Beach. Segrave knew his record would be broken, and said so.

The two Englishmen that helped revive the Battleground of Speed: Campbell (top) standing by his Blue Bird, and Segrave (above) in his Golden Arrow.

One Briton, Two Americans

Next year, sure enough, three challengers attacked Segrave's record. One was another Briton. The other two were Americans. All were veterans of track racing.

First came Capt. Malcolm Campbell. It was he who had driven 174 mph on perilous Pendine Sands shortly before Segrave set the new mark here. Campbell was known as a daredevil on Brooklands track and elsewhere. Yet when I first met him on a Sunday morning in the Ridgewood Hotel lobby, just after his arrival, I thought at first he was one of the mildest men I had ever seen. He spoke so softly; he talked about his car as one would of a pet.

It was characteristic of this remarkable man that he should name his big racer the Blue Bird. Characteristic of him, too, that he carried a medal of St. Christopher, patron saint of travel, on every speed adventure. Soon we learned that the occasional glint in this man's gray eyes had meaning. We learned he was a man of unbridled daring, and as stubborn as they make them.

As soon as his big car was ready to roll, Campbell insisted on taking it to the beach for a trial run – this, despite the warning of AAA officials and others that the speedway just then was in foul shape, but that sooner or later a Northeaster would iron it out. Then when he saw the beach, its surface rippled and marked with shallow pools, he shook his head and said, "I am much disappointed. I was told it was much better than this."

He seemed not to hear when he was told the surface often was bad, but became smooth again. And he seemed not to hear when he was told he shouldn't drive his massive Blue Bird that day. Against all caution he climbed aboard, saying he would make just a trial run. His mechanics pushed him a rolling start. Then he was off south like a bat out of hell.

Police chief Guy Hurd and I followed fast in the chief's car. In no time at all the Blue Bird had gone out of sight behind flying sand and water. Suddenly I had a feeling and I told Hurd I thought he'd better pull to one side. He nodded and turned up to the foot of the dunes. He was none too soon. How Campbell got the Blue Bird turned around I never learned, but here he was coming back, the huge car bellowing and bounding over the uneven beach.

Just opposite where we stood, Campbell hit an especially bad spot. There was a crash that made me think the car was breaking in two. A rooster tail of sand and water spurted 20 feet into the air as the heavy machine sped away. Hurd stood looking after it a moment, then drawled, "He'll get hurt yet if he ain't careful."

Back where Campbell had started on that wild ride we found the mishap had cracked sections of the underslung Blue Bird's shock absorbers. The sheet steel skin on the underside of the body had been stripped loose; it was spread out behind like a dirty wet rag.

Again Campbell complained that the beach was not what he had been told it was. Again we explained, a bit wearily, that it wasn't ready and that he should have waited. The gray-eyed man shook his head and told his crew to take the car back to its garage for repairs.

Meanwhile came one of the American challengers – boyish Frank Lockhart with his 16-cylinder Blackhawk, built to his own design by the Stutz Motor Co. A tiny white car – not black – it had a round body, like a projectile. Its pistons were about the size of a silver dollar. Its supercharger turned up 35,000 revolutions a minute.

Lockhart was one of America's smartest and nerviest track drivers. He was a winner of the Indianapolis 500-mile race. Nearly every dirt and board track in the country knew his heavy foot, his sure hand and eye. (See *Automobile Quarterly* Vol. 44 No. 4, "Genius in the Cockpit.")

But he was bashful, so bashful his beautiful and affectionate wife worried about it. The day his little racer was being unloaded in its garage I tried to interview him, but he only eyed me and edged away – until I exclaimed over the beauty of his car as they stripped its covering off. Then he grabbed me by the arm and began to show it to me, talking like a schoolboy about a new pair of skates.

I saw another side of Britain's Campbell a few days after Lockhart and his Blackhawk arrived.

"It's a beautifully made car and Lockhart is a very brave and able driver," Campbell said to me confidentially. "But the Blackhawk is very light. You need a heavy car for high speeds. I am very fond of Frank. I pray he doesn't have a mishap."

I learned a few days later how deeply the stubborn and fearless Briton meant that when I saw him and Lockhart talking together. Campbell had his arm around the younger man's shoulders. By the look on his face you would have thought it was a father talking to his son. He and Frank became fast friends.

Homemade Monster and Others

After Lockhart came J.M. White, a Philadelphia inventor, and his homemade Triplex. This monster had three 500-horsepower Liberty motors. Its nose was shaped like a chisel. Its tail was broad and blunt. White, too old to drive, had a theory that streamlining was all poppycock – all you

Images of Campbell's Blue Bird in the early 1930s. Campbell broke the land speed record on nine occasions between 1924 and 1935, five times at Daytona Beach. Sir Malcolm died after a long illness in 1949 and was succeeded by his son Donald who continued the record-breaking tradition, breaking 400 mph in the turbine-powered Bluebird CN7 now on loan in Lord Montagu's National Motor Museum at Beaulieu.

needed was a sharp nose to cut the air.

White was looking for a driver. When I asked Cliff Alley, veteran of the Indianapolis Speedway, if he would drive it he looked it over a long time, then turned away and said, "Hell's bells, no."

White was fated not to find a driver or get AAA sanction to enter his monster until later that spring.

Along with the Triplex came a flock of stockcars, their makers and drivers aiming to set new class records. It was a big speed meet, one of the biggest in the beach's history. It was sponsored by the local chamber of commerce, which sold season tickets. Day after day the speed show went on. Spectators came by the thousands.

On Feb. 19, Campbell drove his Blue Bird a mile in 17.39 seconds, 206.95 mph. It was a new world's record. Once again that day Campbell's indomitable will to do things his own way nearly cost him his life. His unhappy experience that first day on the beach had made him wary of the water's edge and wet sand. So, on this day of triumph he drove high up on the beach – almost too high. On the final trip south his right rear wheel hit a bump. We heard the crash, saw Campbell's head pop out of the cockpit, saw him duck back in, swipe his goggles back in place and straighten out the bounding Blue Bird – all in a split second.

Afterward Campbell told us he "nearly spilled." Then he showed us his hands – steady. He was chewing gum. "Ah, yes," he said, "I always chew gum when I drive. American gum. I'm very fond of it, you know."

Talk now turned to Frank Lockhart and his little white car. He had tried it out several times. When he opened it up even part way you could hear the scream of the supercharger for seemingly miles around.

Lockhart's turn would come soon.

Mist on the Windshield

Many events were carded for Washington's Birthday. Some of the best stockcars made in America would be driven over the measured mile by crack professional drivers seeking new class records.

Frank Lockhart and his Blackhawk would be on the course – readied for an all-out attack on the new record set by Campbell only three days earlier. Many thousands came for that holiday event. The stands near the timing station held only a small fraction of the people who had come from miles around, from many cities and many states to watch the day's jousting on the sandy speed arena.

As far as you could see, north and south, there were people. They clustered thickly on the dunes, standing and sitting. Their movements were the movements of a mass. At times you could hear their voices from near and far, a subdued chorus murmur blending with the sound of the surf.

Florida's governor, John Martin, was there with members of his staff. They filled a sizeable space in the middle of the grandstand. Automobiles were parked tightly the length of Atlantic Avenue on both sides, and along the crossroads.

But it was a bad day for the trials, that Feb. 22. The sky was overcast. Mist hung low over the beach. Now and then it turned into a light sprinkle. Despite the weather, many of the stockcar drivers sent their cars barking over the measured mile and back again, but obviously it was no day for a world's record try.

Lockhart brought his tiny Blackhawk out early and stood by, waiting. More than once he had towed his car to the beach but each time something had gone against him. His finely designed racer had to be tuned to perfection, and inevitably faults had shown up that compelled adjustments.

Now, today, his car was ready. So was he, but the weather had turned against him.

We could see him, moodily kicking his toes against one of the tires as officials of the Stutz Motor Car Co. talked to him. We were told they were begging him not to take a chance on his life.

Once, the overcast lifted a little. Lockhart climbed into the narrow cockpit, his crew climbed into the tow car, and the cavalcade rolled to the south end of the course near the Inlet. Then again the weather thickened. The afternoon wore on and the tide began to flow in. Governor Martin and his party left. Some few others followed, believing the day's running was over, but most of the people stayed on the dunes, waiting.

We newspapermen had left the press table and were clustered around Ted Gill, Associated Press correspondent, and his big black sedan parked on the upper margin of the beach. From there we saw men interested in the speed trials promotion hop in a passenger car and drive south. Minutes later we heard the telephone ring in the timing stand. That phone was connected with others at each end of the course and at midway points. Hearing its jingle we agreed it meant Lockhart was telling AAA officials he had given up for the day. We swarmed back to the timing stand, expecting to get the final message and go in with the day's rather meager news report.

T.E. "Pop" Myers, AAA referee and dean of its official staff was talking on the phone. His face was solemn when he put the receiver back and turned to his colleagues. Gravely he and the other officials whispered together; I saw Odis Porter wince. They nodded their heads, then Myers spoke low and carefully to the man who handled the course's only public address system of those days – a huge megaphone.

The megaphone man stared, nodded, then picked up his big horn and turned toward the multitude. His magnified voice boomed over the dunes: "Frank Lockhart will now go for the record."

My station was next to Odis Porter and his electric timer. "What does this mean?" I asked him. He blinked and turned his face away.

This I knew about AAA rules: When a driver of proven experience said he was ready to drive, they let him drive. Lockhart had telephoned he was going for the record. So, despite their fears and deep reluctance, they turned him loose. He was supposed to know what to do.

I turned to Pete Craig, United Press correspondent, who had driven in many barrel turn races on this beach. "It's murder," he whispered.

Again the megaphone man: "Frank Lockhart has started north."

What the Screaming Said

We jumped to the press tables and stared into the mist. We couldn't see anything at first but soon we heard the scream of the supercharger, deep in the gray murk. Then we made out the little car, ghostly white in the fog and running toward us at a speed that seemed fantastic. By the supercharger's crescendo scream we knew Frank was coming with a wide-open throttle. We knew nothing on wheels ever had run as fast as the little white car was running that day.

Then a scarf of light rain drifted across the beach – across the speeding car. Through that thin veil we saw the Blackhawk edging higher on the beach, and higher – too high, into dry sand.

We heard a ringing crash. The car bounded and swerved, skidded diagonally across the beach in two end-for-end loops, and still on its wheels shot nose first into the ocean.

The car ran on its wheels until its belly hit the water. Then miraculously, eerily, like a great white pebble thrown by a superhuman hand it skipped high into the air – high and far. As it soared it made a slow corkscrew turn. At the height of that fearsome leap, when the car was bottom-up, we caught a glimpse of Lockhart's helmeted head. Again the car hit the water, right side up. Again it soared high and far and still a third time.

By now the momentum was broken. Still spinning in a corkscrew whirl, the hapless Blackhawk landed on its wheels, its nose pointed directly toward the shore 200 yards away. A heavy breaker combed over the little racer, all but hiding it from view. A low moan swept the crowd. Nobody there thought Frank Lockhart was alive.

But when the breaker flattened out, Lockhart thrust his hand high out of the cockpit. With one voice thousands of men and women chorused, "He'll drown!" And in one mass they jumped down from the dunes and over the beach.

Something to be remembered was the teamwork that governed the vast mob. Seemingly in seconds trucks were driven to the spot and men swarmed out with cables to pull the racer ashore. Meanwhile, dozens of us ran pell-mell into the water up to our chins and tried to pull Lockhart out of his wreck. But the car's body had been crimped against his groin; he screamed with pain when we yanked at him.

All this while the breakers were curling again and again over the car and Lockhart's head. He would have drowned, surely, had it not been for a happy-go-lucky young man named Gil Farrell. Farrell, a dirt-track driver, climbed upon the headrest behind the cockpit, curled up there and cupped his hands over Lockhart's mouth and nose when the waves broke high. When the breakers flattened out he loosened his hands and yelled, "Now breathe!"

On March 13, 1929, Lee Bible, a Daytonan and short-track racer, in his pursuit for the ultimate speed, paid the ultimate price on his home sands. J.M. White, the rich Philadelphian who owned the Triplex, was on hand with his powerful machine, intent on bringing the title back to America and to his car. Bible made one run, and then attempted another. Just out of the time trap on the record mile, a stretch he made at 202 mph, something went wrong and the car swerved.

By this help Lockhart breathed and thus lived through that adventure. Cables were made fast to the Blackhawk and to trucks on the beach. The racer was pulled into shallow water. The crimped body was straightened out and Lockhart was lifted into a waiting ambulance. Farrell also was put into an ambulance. He was more nearly drowned than Lockhart.

The course engineer measured the length of that

fantastic skid – a half mile.

"Farrell saved my life," Lockhart said at the Halifax Hospital.

Lockhart told us how he happened to drive in that mist. The two men who had driven down to the south end had urged him so persistently to run that they made him angry. So he had started against his best judgment. "Never again," he said, smiling.

The young driver soon recovered from the bad effects of that accident, his worst injury being an injured tendon in the wrist. In a few days his physician, Dr. Guy Klock, said his patient would soon be as good as new. Lockhart announced he would return to Indianapolis, rebuild his battered Blackhawk and come again that spring for another attempt.

Meanwhile, Malcolm Campbell, who had been deeply shocked by Lockhart's mishap, packed up and went back to England with his Napier-powered Blue Bird. The winter trials were over.

Scenes from the last days of Daytona Beach's claim to fame as the world's main speed demon attraction. Here, Campbell prepares for his record-setting run of 276.816 mph in his newest Blue Bird in March 1935. In September of that year, he would reach 301.12 mph at Bonneville Salt Flats, Utah, the new destination for those aspiring to reach yet higher speeds.

Setting Records 'til the End

Malcolm Campbell wasn't allowed to keep his hard-won world's speed record very long. Later that spring J.M. White announced in Philadelphia he had signed a driver for his massive . Ray Keech, also a Philadelphian, who had earned a name for himself on many race tracks, had agreed to drive the big three-motored car as soon as a meet could be arranged. So White asked the AAA to sanction another world's record meet at Daytona Beach in April. The request was granted.

Then, in Indianapolis, Lockhart announced he had rebuilt his white Blackhawk and had completely recovered from his half-mile spill. He would be here also for the April trials.

The contrast between Lockhart and Keech was as marked as the difference between the streamlined little Blackhawk and the ponderous, chisel-nosed Triplex. Lockhart was slender, bashful, boyishly friendly. Keech, an older man, was blocky, tough looking in a way,

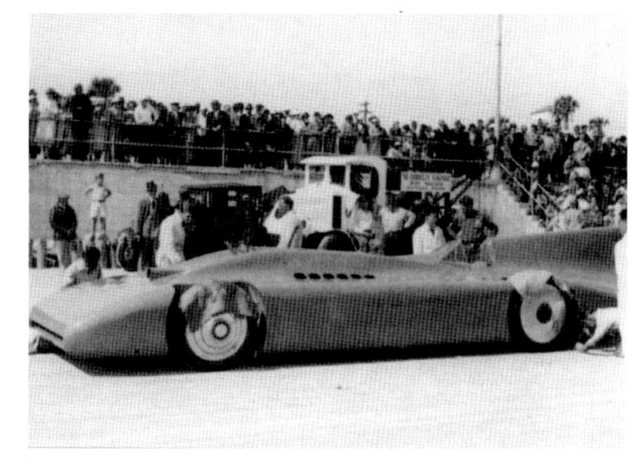

inclined to be moody. But it was Keech who took the new record on April 22, 1928, running at 207.55 mph.

Three days later, it was Lockhart's turn. With a smooth beach and optimal weather, the unthinkable happened – on his third run, failing tire treads led to the horrific, high-speed spectacle that claimed Lockhart's life (see *Automobile Quarterly* Vol. 44 No. 4, "Genius in the Cockpit").

More records were set over the course of the next few years, and another life was lost – Lee Bible, driving White's Triplex. When Campbell returned in 1935 with another upgraded Blue Bird, he drove to a new world's record of 276.816 mph on a sunny March day. He had the power to do better, but the car was badly balanced fore and aft and rocked back and forth at high speed. When Campbell returned to the timing tower after his record run, the rear tires were so deeply frayed that the severed cords spread out on the beach like the fringe of a rug.

Campbell returned home with that record. He never came again. He had learned of a dry salt lake bed in Utah – Bonneville Salt Flats – where he believed greater speeds could be reached. It was there that he captured the coveted record of 300 mph. Since then the Salt Flats have been the stage for world's land speed records.

Daytona Beach had come to the end of an era. It was a great one while it lasted. AQ

AUTOMOTIVE HALL

HONORING THE

Leaders of the Automotive Industry

Consider a world without legends. All the achievements that define industries and even whole societies – the feats, the conquests, the breakthroughs – would be muted. For certain, the heroes of autodom would be relegated to faded memories, eventually lost to time. But thanks to the Automotive Hall of Fame in Dearborn, Mich., no hero of note will ever suffer that demise.

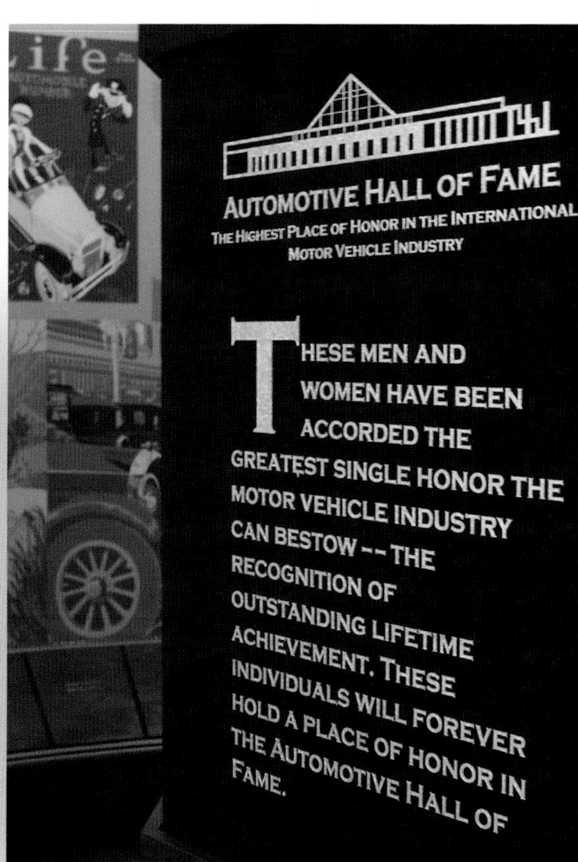

AUTOMOTIVE HALL OF FAME
THE HIGHEST PLACE OF HONOR IN THE INTERNATIONAL MOTOR VEHICLE INDUSTRY
THESE MEN AND WOMEN HAVE BEEN ACCORDED THE GREATEST SINGLE HONOR THE MOTOR VEHICLE INDUSTRY CAN BESTOW -- THE RECOGNITION OF OUTSTANDING LIFETIME ACHIEVEMENT. THESE INDIVIDUALS WILL FOREVER HOLD A PLACE OF HONOR IN THE AUTOMOTIVE HALL OF FAME.

The Automotive Hall of Fame perpetuates far deeper than a mere two-dimensional library of legends. As with other great halls of fame, the legends live on in near-bodily form, and as a result of a vibrant industry-wide effort.

"Our mission is to honor and recognize outstanding achievement in the automotive and related industries," said Jeffrey K. Leestma, president of the Automotive Hall of Fame. "And when you think about it, that's what halls of fame do, whether it be automotive, baseball, football, what have you. We're in the business of recognizing outstanding achievement. And we do that with four separate recognitions."

The first recognition is to be inducted, which was instituted in 1967. Becoming a "hall of famer" first requires the nominee to be either retired from the industry or deceased. Being inducted into the Automotive Hall of Fame is meant to honor a lifetime – or career – achievement, predicated by an extensive review of the inductee's impact on either the automotive industry or the automobile itself.

Over 220 individuals have been inducted into the Automotive Hall of Fame and include such pioneers and leaders as Benz, Bosch, Bugatti, Chevrolet, Chrysler, Citroën, Daimler, Dodge, Durant, Duryea, Ferrari, Ford, Honda, Maybach, Olds, Peugeot, Porsche, Renault, Sloan and Toyoda.

"The second form of recognition is called the Distinguished Service Citation," Leestma said. "This is not only our oldest recognition, but it's most likely the oldest continuous recognition in the industry. We began awarding the Distinguished Service Citation in 1940, a year after the founding of the Automotive Hall of Fame in 1939. The difference between the Distinguished Service Citation and an inductee is that the citation recipients are generally still active in the industry, or are recently retired. But rather than honoring a lifetime achievement, it's really a snapshot year to year of people who are making notable contributions to the industry."

Approximately 400 Distinguished Service Citations have been awarded over the years.

The third recognition is called the Industry Leader of the Year. The award goes to one individual who is generally the head of a large, successful organization. The fourth recognition is called the Young Leadership and Excellence Award, which reflects the Automotive Hall of Fame's commitment to the future by identifying the next generation of leadership in the industry. To be eligible, nominees must be 35 years of age or younger. Just four individuals are honored each year.

Hall of Fame History

The Hall of Fame was founded on Oct. 18, 1939, in New York City. The founders met to create an organization that would perpetuate the memories of the early automotive pioneers as well as the contemporary leaders in the industry.

Much like other halls of fame, the Automotive Hall of Fame is a unique facility where memorabilia is displayed amongst the products of history. Spaces are colorful, bright and informative.

Automotive Hall of Fame Inductees: 1967-2006

1967

Walter P. Chrysler
Henry Ford
Charles F. Kettering
Alfred P. Sloan, Jr.

1968

William C. Durant
Edsel Ford
William S. Knudsen
B.E. "Barney" Oldfield
Ransom E. Olds

1969

Louis Chevrolet
Thomas A. Edison
William E. Holler
Charles E. Wilson

1970

Fred S. Duesenberg
Thomas N. Frost
Louis Schwitzer, Sr.
John W. Stokes
C. Harold Wills

1971

Harlow H. Curtice
Carl G. Fisher
Richard H. Grant
K.T. Keller
Col. Jesse G. Vincent

1972

John W. Anderson
Roy D. Chapin, Sr.
Abner Doble
Herbert H. Franklin
John M. "Jack" Mack

1973

Clessie L. Cummins
Ralph De Palma
Charles E. Duryea
Henry M. Leland
Robert Samuel McLaughlin
Charles Stewart Mott
Edward V. Rickenbacker

1974

Don Allen
David D. Buick
Harvey S. Firestone, Sr.
Walter C. Teagle
Edwin J. Umphrey

1975

Harvey S. Firestone, Jr.
Thomas B. Jeffery
Brouwer D. McIntyre
Charles W. Nash
John l. Wiggins

1976

Carl Breer
E. L Cord

1977

Albert C. Champion
Edward N. Cole
Henry H. Timken, Sr.

1978

Gottlieb Daimler
Charles A. Dana
Rudolf Diesel
Anton "Tony" Hulman, Jr.

1979

Ernest R. Breech
Robert A. Stranahan, Sr.

1980

Willard F. Rockwell, Sr.

1981

Walter F. Carey
Horace E. Dodge
Carlyle Fraser
Martin E. Goldman
J. Irving Whalley

1982

No Inductees

1983

Frederick C. Crawford
Arthur O. Dietz
Joseph O. Eaton
Henry Ford II
Zenon C. R. Hansen

1984

Vincent Bendix
Carl Benz
Robert Bosch
Roy D. Chapin, Jr.
Edward C. Larson
Paul Weeks Litchfield

1985

Edward G. Budd
Heinrich Nordhoff

1986

Harley Earl, Jr.
Fred M. Young, Sr.

1987

Ferdinand Porsche
Wilbur Shaw
Walter W. Stillman

1988

Archie T. Colwell
John W. Koons, Sr.
Hubert C. Moog
Arthur O. Smith
Lloyd R. Smith
Ralph R. Teetor

1989

Gordon M. Buehrig
Soichiro Honda
Frank D. Kent
Elmer H. Wavering

1990

Clarence W. Avery
Charles A. Bott
Philip Caldwell
John E. Goerlich
Thomas A. Murphy
Walter P. Reuther

1991

Zora Arkus-Duntov
J Harwood Cochrane
W. Edwards Deming
Harold D. Draper, Sr.
Rene C. McPherson
Frederick Henry Royce

Automotive Hall of Fame Inductees: 1967-2006 (cont.)

1992

Lee Hunter
Wilton D. Looney
Henry J. Nave
Donald E. Petersen
Charles J. Pilliod, Jr.
James M. Roche
Carroll Shelby

1993

Martin Fromm
Elliot Lehman
William L. Mitchell
Harry C. Stutz

1994

Bela Barenyi
Michael Cardone, Sr.
Fredric G. Donner
Walter E. Flanders
Lee A. Iacocca
Fred Jones
Kenneth W. Self
Eiji Toyoda

1995

Walter O. Bentley
Virgil M. Exner, Sr.
Alfred J. Fisher
Charles T. Fisher
Edward F. Fisher
Fred J. Fisher
Howard A. Fisher
Lawrence P. Fisher
William A. Fisher
Earl Holley
George M. Holley, Sr.
Robert S. McNamara
George W. Romney
Clarence W. Spicer

1996

Frank J. Campbell
Edward Davis
J. Frank Duryea
H.T. Ewald
Wilhelm Maybach
Nicolaus A. Otto
Thomas S. Perry
Freelan O. Stanley
Francis E. Stanley

1997

Joseph R. Degnan
John F. Dodge
Raymond Loewy
Robert B. McCurry
William A. Raftery
Genichi Taguchi
Rollin H. White
Walter C. White
Windsor T. White

1998

Andre Citroën
Yutaka Katayama
Carl Opel
Friedrich Opel
Heinrich Opel
Ludwig Opel
Wilhelm Opel
Charles M. Pigott
Fred M. Zeder
Ferdinand von Zeppelin

1999

Nils Bohlin
Allen K. Breed
Elliot M. Estes
James Ward Packard
William Doud Packard
Armand Peugeot
Harold A. "Red" Poling
Preston Tucker, Sr.

2000

Warren E. Avis
Ettore Bugatti
Enzo Ferrari
Douglas Fraser
August Horch
Wally Parks
Alice Huyler Ramsey

2001

Joe Girard
Denise McLuggage
Ralph Lane Polk II
Charles E. Sorensen
William B. Stout
Roy Warshawsky

2002

Giovanni Agnelli
Giorgetto Giugiaro
Frank E. McCarthy
André Michelin
Edouard Michelin
Richard Petty
Owen R. Skelton

2003

Andy Granatelli
Max Hoffman
Sir Alec Issigonis
Henry B. Joy
J. Edward Lundy
Harry A. Miller
Louis Renault

2004

William France, Sr.
Don Garlits
Donald Healey
J. R. "Pitt" Hyde
Battista Pininfarina
Heinz Prechter
Eberhard von Kuenheim
Jiro Yanase

2005

Mario Andretti
John Boyd Dunlop
Sir William Lyons
Jim Moran
Shirley Muldowney
John F. "Jack" Smith, Jr.
John M. Studebaker
Alexander Winton

2006

Nuccio Bertone
Dale Earnhardt
Bill France, Jr.
H. Wayne Huizenga
Shojiro Ishibashi
Arjay Miller
Bruno Sacco

"The original name of the organization was called the Automobile Old Timers, and when you think about it that's exactly what they were," Leestma said. "In addition to being involved in the auto industry, one of the requirements for the founding members of the organization was that they had to have worked in the industry for at least 20 years. Dating from 1939 and going back 20 years, these gentlemen were involved in the earliest days of the industry."

Leestma concedes, tongue in cheek, that forming the Automobile Old Timers was also an excuse for the founders to sit around hotel lobbies, smoke cigars and talk about the good ol' days. But the organization very quickly formalized. The next year, the first Distinguished Service Citations were awarded to Ransom Olds, Charles King, Charles Henshaw, Julian Chase and Walter Baker. (Baker developed the Baker Electric Car; Chase was an automotive journalist; Henshaw was an engineer and Buick salesman; King was a Detroit auto pioneer; and Ransom Olds, of course, built Oldsmobiles.)

The organization later moved from the Big Apple to Washington, D.C., in 1960. Still without a permanent home, the leaders continued to meet in hotels and other convenient places. Then, in the early 1960s, the board of directors, most with sights set elsewhere, decided to end the endeavor and disperse the assets.

One of the directors, Tom Frost, couldn't quite let it go. Frost, a Ford dealer in Warrenton, Va., appealed to the board that the organization had been honoring the heroes of the industry for more than two decades, and that they had an obligation to keep the faith. Frost then gave the organization its first temporary home on the second floor of a building located on his used car lot in Warrenton. He also hired the first executive director, Dorothy "Dottie" Ross.

"Frost also promised that, within 10 years, they would break ground for a permanent facility," Leestma said. "Sure enough, 10 years later in 1971, they did. They broke ground on the campus of Northwood Institute in Midland, Mich., which is about an hour and a half's drive north of Detroit. There they built the first permanent facility."

The organization called Midland home for 25 years. But the relatively inaccessible location proved inconvenient.

"I suppose if you're sitting in Warrenton, Va., which is about 50 miles west of Washington, and looking at a map, you may think that Midland was a suburb of Detroit. The fact is, it was too far off the beaten path."

This contention was proven in low foot traffic. The Midland location saw only about 200 visitors a year. According to Leestma, the lights would be turned on only when a visitor happened upon the property.

That prompted the board of directors to focus on relocating the facility to Detroit. The present Automotive Hall of Fame building, in Dearborn, was opened 10 years ago on Aug. 17, 1997.

The focus and purpose of the Automotive Hall of Fame is the people that made the industry great. Here we find the only industry-wide means to honor the men and women of the global motor vehicle and related industries.

Creative promotions have helped make the hall of fame a success. To the right is a gift shop coupon commemorating Ford's famous pay raise.

It was a wise move: today, the Automotive Hall of Fame welcomes nearly 30,000 visitors a year.

"We also get about 200 school classrooms a year," Leestma said. "They are hosted free of charge. In addition to being part of our educational mission, we think it's important to get young people excited about the auto industry."

In 2007, the Hall of Fame will host three workshops in conjunction with the College for Creative Studies in Detroit, one of the major training grounds for automobile designers. The college will set up shop, where students age 10-15 can participate in design workshops. Instruction will basically consist of rudimentary design and drawing techniques.

"You never know what's going to spark something in a child," Leestma said. "We may bring in 100 kids, and if only one or two get that spark, it has all been worthwhile."

On Display

The kids come in and are exposed to the heroes of the industry," Leestma said. "I often make the comparison between what we do and Cooperstown, the Baseball Hall of Fame. People understand what that's all about. When I say that we're the Cooperstown of the auto industry, people understand what we do."

Walking through the Hall of Fame provides an impressive array of unique artifacts. Many items are one of a kind, such as the last remaining pair of "chicken farmer" coveralls worn by Carroll Shelby during his early racing days. Donations from the "old timers" began in earnest as far back as the '40s.

Leestma, who also wears the hat of curator for the Hall of Fame's automobile and memorabilia collection, typically approaches inductees for donations or artifact loans. What better way for visitors to experi-

ence the inductee and their career than to see their personal contribution in the form of a helmet, goggles, car model or other piece of history.

"People don't go to Cooperstown to learn about Babe Ruth or Mickey Mantle or Hank Aaron; they really go there to see the artifacts, the gloves, the jerseys, the bats, the shoes," Leestma said. "We're no different. It's a physical connection."

When Richard Petty was inducted four years ago, Leestma asked Petty if there was anything he could send. Not knowing what to expect, the Hall of Fame received Petty's cowboy hat and sunglasses, a perfect representation of the NASCAR giant's persona. Behind a glass case, the display has become one of the most popular.

"People will stand and look at that case for the longest time," Leestma said. "Again, it's the physical connection. It's the next best thing to him being there."

Seeing Petty's display, Carroll Shelby also sent his trademark black hat, which now accompanies his coveralls.

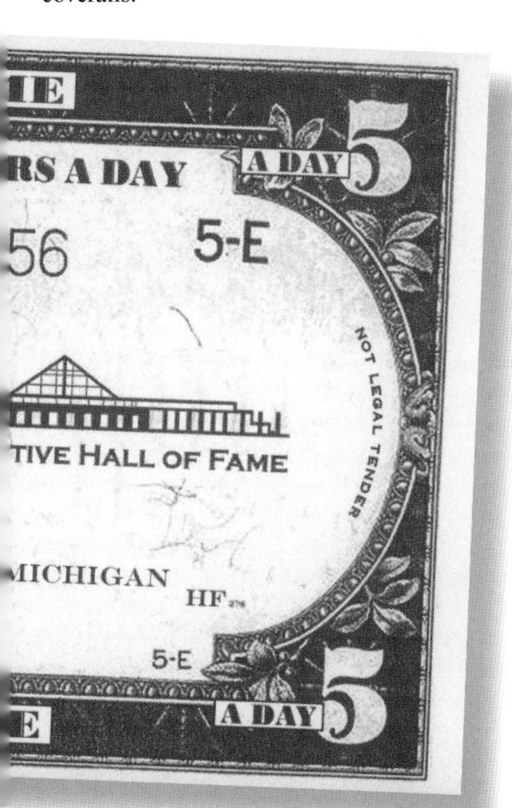

The history of mobility is preserved by celebrating the creativity, toil and genius of the individual. Displays are graphical and educational resources.

Maximizing Its Clout

The Hall of Fame's bylaws allow for up to 50 members to sit on the board. There is currently just under that number. Board members hold titles that run the gamut of the industry, from OEM firms to aftermarket specialists to retailers. The Hall of Fame is dependent upon the auto industry as a whole for its ongoing operation; about 60 percent of its operating budget comes from corporate, foundation and individual support.

"They support us because they believe in our mission," Leestma said. "Our supporters believe that it is important that we remember and honor the heroes."

Functioning as a non-profit 501(c) 3, the Automotive Hall of Fame offers its accommodations to companies and organizations for conferences and meetings. Roughly 10,000 square feet of unique spaces, such as a 68-seat theater, a luxurious executive conference room, dinner seating for up to 120 and reception accommodations for up to 400, the Hall of Fame is an ideal venue for corporate meetings or events. (Another 10,000 square feet is devoted to museum space.)

The scope of historical coverage is great, from technical innovation to personal "artifacts" as seen to the right with Carroll Shelby's last pair of overalls worn while racing. Shelby would come straight from his chicken farm to race.

"Any company can hold an event at a hotel, one of those bland ballroom-like conference rooms," Leestma said. "But to hold an event at the Hall of Fame can take an event to the next level."

The unique construction of the building was intentional. The directors wanted to attract people to use the Hall of Fame for several type of events: breakfast meetings, dinner receptions, product walk-arounds, audio/visual presentations, press conferences, new vehicle introductions. The Atrium, Theater, Styling Gallery and Conference Room are unique venues for daytime or evening meetings or for entertaining guests. In the warmer months, people can host their outdoor event on the landscaped courtyard, which can accommodate 100 people.

Directors and staff give teaching the next generation a top priority. The goal is to inspire individuals to higher levels of achievement in their own lives.

Guests are invited to stroll through the Hall of Fame's exhibits during special events where they can experience interactive displays and authentic artifacts about the global automotive industry, its pioneers, inventors, innovators and leaders.

"One of the key messages I want visitors – especially the kids – to take with them, when they look at all these heroes, all these automotive greats, is that they weren't born great," Leestma said. "They achieved greatness through inspiration, through vision, and through hard work. At some point in their lives they were inspired by someone or something. Once they got that spark of inspiration, they created their own vision as to where they wanted to take it. And of course the hard work is necessary.

"The role of the Hall of Fame is to provide that spark."

Around the World

Bretislav B.P. de

n a Skoda

ubé’s Borghese-Inspired Adventure

When Bretislav B. P. de Dubé drove his dusty, navy blue Skoda into Prague on July 31, 1936, and pulled to a stop in front of the Czech Automobile Club’s headquarters on Lützow Street (now Opletalova Street), he became the first motorist to complete a 360-degree trip around the world, ending his journey at precisely the same spot where he had begun it a little more than two months earlier. Covering 17,000 overland miles (27,700 km) in 97 days, he made the record-setting trip in his personal car—a 1936 production-model Skoda Rapid Kabriolet.

BY ALISON TARTT

De Dubé's achievement – along with the Skoda's gritty endurance – was soon forgotten with the outbreak of war in Europe, but the journey had its impetus in one of the great events in the history of motor sports: the epic Peking-to-Paris rally of 1907. Since boyhood, when young Bretislav had met the legendary Prince Borghese, a friend of his father's, and heard about the count's adventure, he had longed to undertake a similar expedition.

Purchased by de Dubé in the spring of 1936, the car was a two-door, rear-axle-drive model with a four-cylinder, 1.5-liter 38hp engine, three-speed transmission, Scintilla Vertex ignition, Solex carburetor, Champion spark plugs, and Matador Mamut tires. Factory-assembled on April 11, just two weeks before the departure date of April 25, the Skoda was fitted with a jumbo gas tank in the trunk, which allowed it to travel about a thousand miles without refueling. The gas tank and the magneto ignition were the only modifications for the grueling trip ahead.

Tidewater Petroleum, producer of Tydol and Veedol products, served as the chief sponsor of the trip; Philips donated a radio receiver. In addition to water, canned goods and other provisions (including tins of chocolate from a Czech confectioner), cameras and binoculars, and a first aid kit with morphine, de Dubé packed two handguns and a submachine gun for possible encounters with bandits. With the necessary visas and letters of introduction in hand, de Dubé set out for Russia by way of Germany, Poland, Lithuania, and Latvia, accompanied by Jindrich Kubias, a close friend and a trained mechanic.

At the Russian border, the Skoda was not allowed to proceed except with a Russian soldier as an escort, as the authorities regarded two Czechs on a junket as highly suspicious. As likely spies, they were not allowed to travel during daylight hours. Despite these constraints, de Dubé and Kubias were the first motorists permitted to drive a privately owned car across Russia. The usual trans-Russia travelers were compelled to ship their transport by rail to a specific

Top: Bretislav B.P. de Dubé (behind the wheel) and Jindrich Kubias (standing) set out for a trip around the world, traversing the globe east to west, beginning in their homeland Czechoslovakia. Left: De Dubé (center) stands out in the gathering of shorter men during their stop at the Czechoslovak Embassy in Teheran. Right: The Skoda attracts a crowd in Lahore.

destination. Because there were few roads (usually consisting of straw and mud) and no bridges, they often traveled on railway tracks. On one occasion, they experienced a rollover in the Skoda when they were forced over a steep railroad embankment to avoid an oncoming train.

Originally de Dubé planned to go through Russia east into Mongolia and then to China, but border clashes made a change in the route prudent. Furthermore, travel in Russia was proving more expensive than anticipated: food and lodging were costing more than what the best Paris hotels could offer, and each bucket of bathwater was an extra charge.

From Moscow, de Dubé turned southward, driving to Rostov and then Baku. At Pahlavi, the Skoda became the first car to enter Iran at the Caspian port Pahlavi (now Bandar-e Anzali). Crossing the Persian deserts, de Dubé and Kubias discovered that they were more comfortable in the intense heat if all the car windows were tightly closed. The roads, made of a macadam substance over wood, became so soft at times that they had to wait for the surface to harden to avoid getting stuck. They reached the Pakistan border in about 50 hours, then lost their way in a sandstorm near Quetta, which wasted two valuable days.

Determined to finish the trip within 100 days, de Dubé and Kubias traveled by steamer from Bombay to Penang, then by ferry to Malaya. From here they drove through the jungle to Singapore, where they boarded a ship to Hong Kong. Sino-Japanese tensions made it risky to drive through China, so they continued by ship to Shanghai and then on to Kobe, where they were again suspected of being spies, their binoculars and cameras raising alarms among the Japanese officials. They crossed the Pacific via Honolulu.

When de Dubé and Kubias reached San Francisco, they had left most of the trip's challenges behind them. Good roads and an abundance of service stations lay ahead. Yet they had experienced only minor mechanical problems with the Skoda – primarily punctures and broken springs. The engine had never missed a beat.

As they crossed the United States, their main concern was now keeping to a timetable. Along the way,

In India: The two Czech world travelers upon their arrival in Bombay. The men wanted to help put the Czechoslovak state—then less than two decades old—on the world map. De Dubé's son, Bret, recently said in an interview: "Many times they slept in the car, and they bought supplies on the way if they could. But they had canned goods, they had even chocolate in a can ... and they had canned water, cans of water, because they went through the desert."

At a San Francisco service station, a first chance to have the Skoda Rapid serviced. Above: Mr. Shawkem, a AAA representative with a road map planning the best road to take through North America.

automobile clubs feted them with receptions, usually calling for de Dubé to give a speech, so he and Kubias often drove around the clock to make up for lost time.

In New York, on July 22, they were the guests of honor at a luncheon held at the Lexington Hotel by the Automobile Club of America, one of the founding member organizations of the American Automobile Association. Elmer Thompson, the club's secretary, presented a gold medal to de Dubé, along with a silver map of the world. The next day, Cunard's R.M.S. *Berengaria* transported the Skoda and its drivers to Cherbourg, France, where the two motorists set out for Paris and then began the final leg to Prague. At Czechoslovakia's border, Skoda Works had assembled 100 company cars to escort de Dubé and Kubias to the capital city.

A full seven decades later de Dubé's son, Bret Prochazka, has clear memories of that day when his father and Kubias finally arrived in front of the Prague Auto Club, from where they had set out 97 days previously. He told Ian Willoughby of Radio Praha:

"I was 11 years old and I'll never forget that, because there were thousands of people in front and we arrived and we couldn't get to the building. We had a police escort so that we could get through and I could embrace my father after not seeing him for three months."

The Western India Automobile Association publication recorded the state of the car upon the trip's completion: "A diary written during the trip is interesting. The front spring had to be repaired 18 times, out of this no less than 16 times in Russia, once in Iran and once in China ... tyres had to be repaired 22 times, mostly in Russia. Out of the total six tyres, four originals completed the trip. The original set of sparking plugs was used throughout; and one ignition cable was replaced on account of faulty insulation."

Remarkably, de Dubé kept the Skoda as the family car until after the war, when it was confiscated by the government. In 1938 he published a book about his adventure, "Automobilem Kolem Sveta (Around the World by Car)", which has yet to be translated into English. AQ

Above: George Eyston and de Dubé aboard the *Berengaria*, July 1936. Eyston was returning to London shortly after breaking several land speed records in his "Speed of the Wind" racer at Bonneville Salt Flats. Below: De Dubé presenting a scale model of the Apollo Lunar Landing Module to the National Technical Museum in Prague on behalf of Grumman Corporation, 1970.

Bretislav B. P. de Dubé

Born into an aristocratic Bohemian family in Prague in 1898, Bretislav B. P. de Dubé took an early interest in automobiles. After studying mechanical engineering at Prague Polytechnic, de Dubé worked during World War I at Josef Walter's factory, a motorcycle and three-wheeler manufacturer that had begun building cars in Jinonice. Following stays in France and the United States, de Dubé returned to Europe as a manager for a Manhattan-based importer, Penn Commercial Corp. of America (previously Czechoslovak Commercial Corp. of America). In 1930 he and his brother Josef purchased a factory in the old Prague neighborhood of Smíchov, where they established the city's first modern garage, Autoclub Garáže. By this time, de Dubé was known as Bretislav Jan Procházka, having adopted a Czech name in the nationalistic postwar climate of the newly established Czechoslovakia. For a time, he was associated with the Skoda company in Prague as a consulting engineer.

Active in motor sports, de Dubé participated in races and rallies in both the United States and Central Europe, accumulating a collection of trophies and badges. He also served on the Sporting Committee of the Automobile Club of Czechoslovakia and officiated at races in Monte Carlo. His close friends included automotive journalist Charles Faroux, racing drivers George Eyston and Elisabeth Junek, and Tatra designer Hans Ledwinka. As a motor sports correspondent and car expert, de Dubé wrote for Czechoslovakia's largest newspaper, *Polední List Express*, as well as such magazines as *Auto*, *Auto Bild*, *Der Motor*, and *La Vie Automobile*.

In 1948, following the seizure of his garage by Czechoslovakia's communist regime, he emigrated to the United States and started a flight information company, SignaTronic, in East Elmhurst, New York. A life member of the Sports Car Club of America and the Society of Automotive Engineers, he authored (with Marcel Reichel) a biography of Charles Kettering, "Boss Ket: La Vie d'un Grand Inventeur"; a car repair and service guide, "Motormaster"; and articles for various car magazines. Two of his articles appeared in *Automobile Quarterly* in 1969.

On Oct. 29, 1971, at the age of 74, Bretislav de Dubé died in an automobile accident outside Washington, D.C.

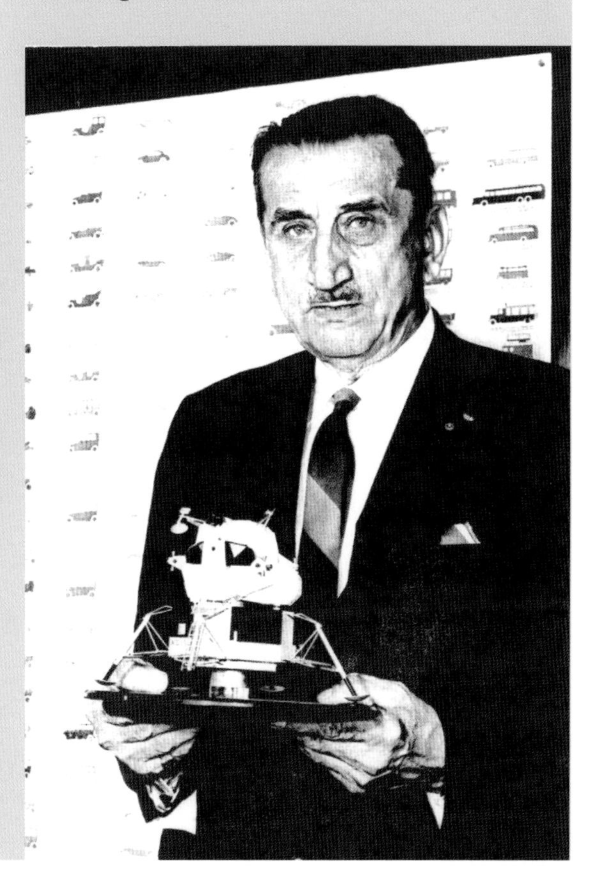

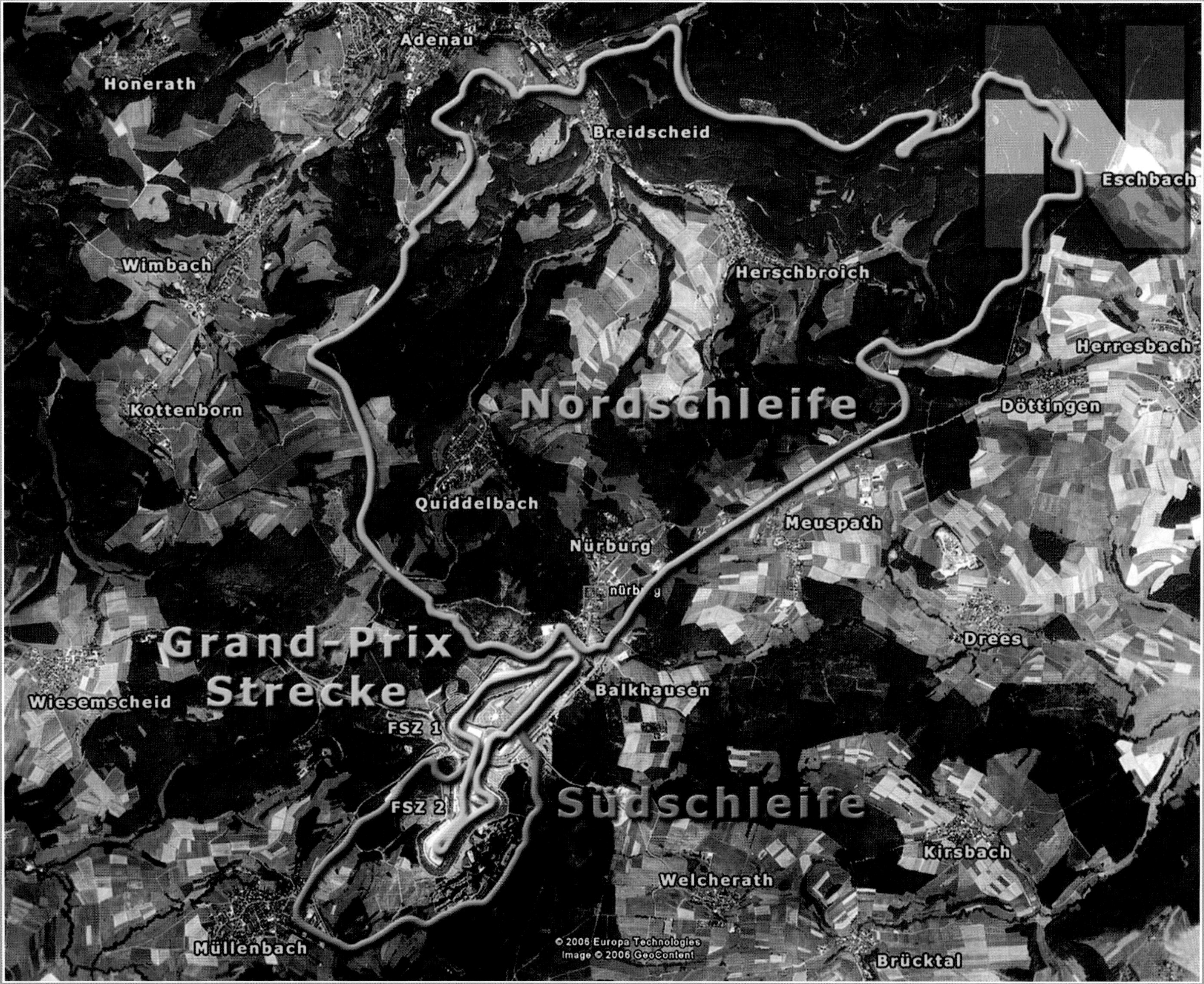
Adenau
Honerath
Breidscheid
Eschbach
Wimbach
Herschbroich
Herresbach
Nordschleife
Döttingen
Kottenborn
Quiddelbach
Meuspath
Nürburg
nürburg
Grand-Prix
Strecke
Drees
Balkhausen
Wiesemscheid
FSZ 1
FSZ 2
Südschleife
Kirsbach
Welcherath
Müllenbach
© 2006 Europa Technologies
Image © 2006 GeoContent
Brücktal

Lords of the Ring

There is a bucolic section of Germany's mountainous Eifel region, stretching from the Rhine to the Belgian border, that is home to medieval castles surrounded by forested hills and sun-drenched valleys. But in a corner of this countryside is a winding patch of pavement upon which the rumble of racing has broken the quietness for 80 years. They call it the Nürburgring, or as one driver once labeled it, "The green hell."

BY RANDY BARNETT

Germany's majestic Nürburgring circuit, with a harrowing one-lap distance of 14.2 miles, stands as a salute to the glory days of grand prix racing. The 80-year-old track, which once hosted the German Grand Prix on an annual basis, lost that honor in 1976 when the reigning world champion Niki Lauda crashed heavily there in his Ferrari. The Austrian driver suffered near-fatal burn injuries but battled back to race only a few weeks later in the Italian Grand Prix. It was a brave and gutsy drive.It all happened during the fabled 1976 Formula One grand prix campaign, one that ended with England's James Hunt beating Lauda for the world title by just one point in a highly dramatic Japanese Grand Prix – the final race of the season.

The old Nürburgring (there's a new, much shorter one in use now) was the most demanding and challenging circuit in the world, one that had taken the lives of many brave drivers. It was a genuine "driver's course," where a superior driver in a so-so car could beat a good driver in a superior car. On the Nürburgring ("Ring" for short), driving brilliance was what it was all about.

Scotland's Jackie Stewart, who won there three times once said, "The driver wins here, and it is a special distinction. But it's a treacherous and difficult track, and more than once I said to myself 'Thank God' when I had finished a race there."

America's Mario Andretti, practicing on the Nürburgring for the first time in a works Lotus during the 1969 German Grand Prix, said, "This is what I call a real he-man's circuit."

As American drivers once considered their careers incomplete until they had won the Indianapolis 500, the same attitude prevailed among grand prix drivers where the old Nürburgring was concerned. If you hadn't won the German Grand Prix on the Ring, your career in Formula One racing had not been fulfilled.

Many racing fans still assume that the illustrious Nürburgring was a concept of Adolf Hitler, aiming to impress the world with the achievements of his Nazi regime and to display the superiority of German cars. But this was not the case. The building of the Ring took place long before Hitler came to power.

The Ring was constructed primarily for economic reasons, to combat unemployment and to create a business climate that would help alleviate poverty in the lonely Eifel Mountain region, a heavily forested area south of Cologne. Construction of the gigantic circuit began in the spring of 1925, with the work completed in 1927, six years before Hitler's Nazi party took control of Germany.

The first race staged on the Ring – the "Internationalen Eifelrennen" – took place on the weekend of June

Left: Bernd Rosemeyer is applauded by the crowd after winning the German Grand Prix at Nürburgring in 1936 in his Auto Union. Rosemeyer went on to win the European Drivers' Championship that year, winning the Swiss and Italian Grands Prix as well. Right: Stirling Moss takes the checkered flag at the 1961 German Grand Prix in his Lotus 18/21-Climax.

Above: A Jaguar Mk II in action during a 1963 six-hour race at the Ring. Right: The Ford GT goes through inspection at Nürburgring for its first race in 1964.

18-19, 1927. It was a huge success, with more than 200,000 spectators pouring into the Eifels. More successes would follow, and except for two races in Berlin and one at Hockenheim, the Ring would remain the "home" of the German Grand Prix through 1976, when an era ended. The Ring was a victim of progress, according to some German officials, and a victim of cowardice, according to others. It all depended on who you talked to within German motorsports circles. Regardless, the German Grand Prix was moved to the Hockenheim circuit near Heidelberg in 1977, the year after Lauda's crash.

The Old Ring

The old Nürburgring is still used by the German auto industry for testing and there's also touring car racing. It's also open for a fee to auto and cycle enthusiasts to drive on. In its grand prix days, the old track was 14.2 miles to the lap, as noted earlier, and it had a total of 73 curves – 33 lefts and 40 rights – all of them difficult and many of them blind. The course ran uphill and downhill, with little in the way of flat, straight track.

It featured a change in elevation of nearly 1,000 feet – the high point the start/finish line at 2,046 feet and the low point of Breidscheid at 1,056. The steepest rise is 17 percent, with the steepest decline a hair-raising 27 percent. The famous Karussel or "merry-go-round," a deep-dish bowl that pounded suspensions mercilessly, was a favorite viewing area.

When Eifel weather is fair, the Nürburgring and the area it runs through is beautiful. But when the weather turns foul, and that condition prevails there often, the place becomes a horror for drivers and spectators alike.

Australian Paul Hawkins, who competed on the Ring often, summed it up in May 1968 when he was driving a Ford GT40 there with Jacky Ickx of Belgium in a world championship 1,000-kilometer race for sports cars. The weather that weekend was of the typical Nürburgring variety.

"Bloody awful place, this is," Paul said, during a

Left: The Ford GT during a rainy pit stop at the 1964 Nürburgring 2000K. Right: Phil Hill in the Ford GT passes a Cobra, No. 99, on the outside during the contest.

break in the driving. "In just one lap it was dry, turned to wet, and up around Hohe Acht I ran into a snowstorm. And in May, mind you. Can you believe it? Then farther on rain and finally dry again. All in one lap, mind. It's a crazy place."

But crazy or not, a top driver accepted its challenges. A victory there was, indeed, "a special distinction," as Jackie Stewart so aptly put it.

Epic grand prix races were run on the Ring long before World War II, and long afterward. The greatest prewar grand prix came in 1935 when the legendary Italian driver Tazio Nuvolari, in an outclassed and outdated Alfa Romeo, turned back the might of Mercedes and Auto Union to take the checkered flag.

Another classic came in 1957 when Argentina's aging "Maestro" Juan Manuel Fangio came from far behind to beat the young English drivers Mike Hawthorne and Peter Collins. In that race, Argentina's Fangio, age 46 and driving a Maserati, beat the Englishmen who drove far superior Ferrari cars for the all-conquering Italian team. Fangio, whose favorite track was the Ring, won there three times during his long and distinguished career, and considered his 1957 drive the best of his life.

In the 1968 German Grand Prix, another epic run came when Jackie Stweard, driving a Tyrrell-Ford, won in the worst weather conditions possible, many sections of the track totally awash. Stewart, who never put a wheel wrong in the heavy fog and rain, beat England's Graham Hill that day by some four minutes.

"I will always recall that race," Stewart once said, "a race where I couldn't see anything except walls of spray until I finally got the lead. Even thinking of that race still scares me. But it was my best technical drive, and I consider it my greatest victory."

Along with its fame for horrendous weather conditions, the old Ring's geographical situation provided another interesting element. Its location was unique in the history of motor sport, with its starting area located within view of the village of Nürburg. There, an enormous 11th century castle brooded down over the noisy and dangerous proceedings.

A circuit of such magnitude and grandeur can never again be duplicated, simply because of property costs in today's world. Nor would the modern grand prix car, built for relatively smooth surfaces, be able to run on it. For mile after mile, grand prix cars of yesteryear ran uphill and down, and it ran near villages of medieval origin. Surfaces were bumpy and treacherous.

Of course, track conditions and the circuit environs enriched the spectators' experience all the more. Crowds that stood at anywhere from 250,000 to 300,000 came to see the German Grand Prix at the Ring. And in the 1950s, when cars and gasoline were scarce in postwar Germany, people walked or rode bicycles to get there. Once there, camping along the track was "the only way to go" for the die-hard racing fan, and the whole grand prix week provided for a summer "beer bacchanal" deluxe. Partying was all part of the deal. On the night before a grand prix, thousands of campfires dotted the landscape and tents lined every foot of the area behind the racetrack.

The Ring more than fulfilled its original aim, which was to bring prosperity to the Eifels. Fine hotels and charming "gasthouses" located within 30 miles of the circuit did enormous business on weekends of grand prix races. And business was almost as good during World Championship 1,000 kilometer races for sports car prototypes. The German Grand Prix motorcycle races, Formula 2 races and major touring car events also brought in big money to the Eifel Mountain area.

The German GP Moves

But all things pass, and despite the Ring's great success and international fame, it died in 1976, only one year before what would have been its 50th anniversary. As previously noted, the primary cause of its death was Lauda's crash.

Above: The 1966 German Grand Prix comes to order. John Surtees in his Cooper T81-Maserati, 2nd position, leads Lorenzo Bandini in a Ferrari 312, 6th position. Behind Bandini is Jack Brabham in his Brabham BT19-Repco, 1st position. Below: Denny Hulme in his Brabham BT24-Repco, 1st position, passes Jackie Stewart and his retired BRM P83 during the German Grand Prix, Aug. 6, 1967.

Leading big that year for a possible second straight world championship, Lauda hated the Nürburgring. And he wasn't the only one. He was, however, its most outspoken critic. A few other drivers – such as Sweden's Ronnie Peterson, Belgium's Jacky Ickx and Switzerland's Clay Regazzoni – revered the challenges that the great old circuit offered, and they defended it as the grand prix site. Both Ickx and Regazzoni had won there, and the circuit had provided Jackie Stewart with three of his finest grand prix victories. But by '76, those who promoted the track were clearly the minority.

The Ring had been in big trouble long before Lauda's accident. In 1970, the circuit came under heavy criticism because of its lack of safety standards, and the race that year was switched to the flat and featureless stadium circuit at Hockenheim. The driver boycott of the 1970 German Grand Prix had sent a clear message to Nürburgring officialdom, and it did not go unnoticed elsewhere. It was the beginning of the end for most of the classic European circuits.

Moving the German Grand Prix to Hockenheim that year provoked outrage from many quarters, *MotorSport Magazine* among them. Their famous correspondent Denis Jenkinson, a sharp critic of the Ring boycott,

Ford took top honors at the 1968 1000K race. Above: Paul Hawkins (left) and Jacky Ickx (right) on the victory rostrum after winning in their GT-40 (below).

skipped the grand prix at Hockenheim and covered a Formula 2 race that day at the Ring instead.

"I could only get away with something like that once," Jenks said, "but it gave me a great deal of satisfaction to make a protest like that."

After the boycott, Nürburgring officials launched a complete and expensive renovation of the old track. The work took place in late 1970 and early '71, with the German Grand Prix safely back in place for its August '71 running. Yet while the nearly $2 million renovation work (more runoff area, guardrails, etc.) was widely praised, it did not take any clairvoyance to see that it was primarily a holding action. No matter what steps officialdom took, the Ring was doomed, the end only a matter of time.

In 1975, the year before Lauda's accident, South Africa's Jody Scheckter had said, "The Nürburgring is just too bloody dangerous. If you go off at speed on a downhill section they shouldn't bother to call the ambulance. They wouldn't find the pieces. We are racers, not daredevils, and I like to look at racing as a sport."

Sweden's Ronnie Peterson, who died of injuries received in a crash at the 1978 Italian Grand Prix, described the Ring's plight best. During an interview before the '76 German Grand Prix, Peterson said: "I like to drive here. A lot of others like to drive here, and I would even include Niki Lauda among them. It's

the most exciting and challenging place in the world to drive.

"But the safety problem just can't be solved, it seems. If you have an accident, it takes too long for anyone to reach you. On a normal track, there's always help only 50 meters away. I know they have rescue units all around the Nürburgring, but there are always problems of some kind."

(Peterson was prophetic here. It took rescue cars several minutes to reach Lauda, and it was Lauda's fellow drivers, not rescue workers, who freed him from his burning Ferrari.)

"So the safety factor is the main thing," Peterson said. "Then comes today's grand prix cars. These cars aren't designed for a track like the Ring with all its jumps. The fact is, most of today's cars are designed to run on dance floors. The cars have hardly any ground clearance. They break here where they wouldn't break anywhere else. The Nürburgring is one of my favorite circuits, but times change and like it or not, the Ring will give way."

The German Grand Prix at the Nürburgring for 1976 had become an issue as early as February when Max Mosley, then a spokesman for the Formula One Constructors Association, promised the Automobile Club of Germany that the association would honor its contract to race there for that year's grand prix. But a grand prix at Hockenheim was in mind for the future, with Mosley saying, "We would much prefer to have the race at Hockenheim this year because it's easier working there, but we will honor our 1976 contract for the Nürburgring."

In May, the circuit was inspected by FIA officials and they declared it fit for the German Grand Prix and for future grands prix there, for that matter. "There's absolutely no reason why the German Grand Prix can't continue to be held here," one of the inspectors stoutly maintained.

But defending world champion Lauda disputed the FIA inspection team's findings. Lauda continued his vociferous attacks on the Nürburgring as unsafe for both drivers and spectators.

Unlike most other tracks in Europe, the Nürburgring

Niki Lauda (left) making his opinion known before the 1976 German Grand Prix. His Ferrari 312T2 before (above) and after his near-fatal accident, August 1976. It would prove the end of grand prix racing at the Ring as it had been known for decades.

had a German mystique of its own as well as thousands of loyal and fanatical supporters. And they all dispised Lauda for his criticisms of Germany's racing "holy of holies." When Lauda suffered rib injuries that fateful summer in a tractor accident while working on the yard of his home, the Germans had a field day, saying, "Since the world champion doesn't even know how to drive a tractor without hurting himself, what could he possibly know about safety on the Nürburgring?"

More jokes followed, but Lauda would eventually get even.

Going into the '76 German Grand Prix, many top racing people hinted that it would be the 49th and last one on the Nürburgring, no matter what FIA inspectors would rule now or in the future. Entrenched German officialdom saw otherwise, many already discussing plans for a gala 50th running in 1977.

For the '76 race, the majority of drivers agreed with Lauda and raced against their will and better judgment. From the large starting field, it was truly ironic that Lauda, who had led the attack, crashed and burned on a circuit he hated so much. Along with dooming the Ring, his accident cost him a second straight world championship. He had led the Englishman Hunt by a big points margin going into the race, but Hunt won

The mystique of Nürburgring lingers. Where better to test new models, such as Cadillac's CTS-V, than the twisting turns and terrain of the Ring.

while Lauda fought for his life in a hospital. As noted earlier, Lauda bravely returned to the fray at the Italian Grand Prix only four weeks later despite his injuries. But he finally lost his title to Hunt in the final race of the '76 season in Japan.

Although the issue of the German Grand Prix at the Nürburgring appeared dead after Lauda's accident, both Nürburgring officials and the Automobile Club of Germany mounted a strong campaign to stage a 50th anniversary running in '77. In February of that year, the sponsoring Automobile Club of Germany came out fighting, stating it would not back down to anyone. "Those who want to race for money and world championship points on the Ring this year may do so," the club said, "and those who want to stay away should stay away."

The club added that the race would not go to Hockenheim as it had in 1970.

Martin Urbanus, the boss of the Nürburgring's total operation, attacked the Formula One drivers as irresponsible and "money mad." He also charged that the constructors were making cars that were unsafe and technically inadequate. In his assault, Urbanus charged, "Despite the most modern technical improvements at the Nürburgring, the drivers complain about the natural difficulty of the circuit. But at the same time, they accept without complaint the potentially catastrophic conditions at certain other

circuits ... Monaco, Fuji, Mosport and Long Beach. Is it just lack of insight, or is it the high starting money that prompts the drivers to start these races?

"Until now, world-famous drivers have accepted the challenge of the Nürburgring and have considered a victory on this circuit as the high point of their careers. The whining from Niki Lauda and most of today's drivers shows just how inadequate they really are when compared to the men of the past."

Despite the defensive stands from Urbanus and the Automobile Club of Germany, and from the Ring's thousands of fans who placed "Save the Nürburgring" decals on their cars, the old Nürburgring now faced its end as the site of the German Grand Prix.

In the spring of 1977, Lauda and fellow Formula One driver John Watson of Northern Ireland made an official but cursory inspection of the Ring, and quickly declared it unsafe and unfit to race on. Their decision had the full support of the reigning world champion James Hunt, and most – but not all – of the other drivers.

So the grand prix was moved to Hockenheim for good, and the old Ring faded into obscurity.

Ironically, Lauda won the German Grand Prix at Hockenheim in 1977, exactly one year after his near-fatal accident on the Nürburgring. After winning, he said, "Every victory is special, but to win here in Germany today is a truly special victory for me."

Perhaps it was, as well as revenge for all of the animosity the German fans had heaped upon him as a driver. Still, Austria's Lauda would never achieve that one "special victory" – to take the checkered flag in the German Grand Prix on the awesome and unforgiving Nürburgring circuit. AQ

Racing is back at the Ring, albeit on a shorter course. Left: Formula One action at the 2002 European Grand Prix. Above: Michael Schumacher on the podium after the 2006 European Grand Prix.

Editor's note: Today, there is a "new" Nürburgring, a much smaller circuit consisting of 3.2 miles and which opened for grand prix action in 1984. When the new version of the circuit was revealed it was obvious that the only thing it had in common with the original was a name: Its clinical design, with unchallenging corners and huge run-off areas gave it a soulless feel. Alain Prost won the first event in 1984 when the circuit staged the European Grand Prix. After a one-off outing in 1985 as the German Grand Prix the circuit remained unused for F1 events until 1995 when it became a regular feature of the Grand Prix calendar as either the Grand Prix of Luxembourg or Europe. Although the facilities are excellent and recent years have provided for some entertaining races, racing historians point out that the new Ring can never be more than a tame copy of its older brother.

DALLAS
2001
14
RICCI
26

Shirley's Stable

Horse lovers come in many stripes. There are those who admire horses from a distance, while they gallop at speed or nimbly perform at a steeplechase. Then there are those who esteem horses from the saddle, and the ensuing friendship between man and beast is marked by fondness and respect. Jon Shirley is of the latter crowd, as his stable of prancing horses attests.

PHIL BERG

Jon Shirley's interest "is in Ferraris, from the time I first rode in one." Shirley owns one of the largest collections of very rare Ferraris, which he has acquired in the past two decades. "I like dual-purpose cars, ones that can be raced and have a significant racing history, and also be driven to the track on the street or around town for shopping errands. I like a great racing history. That's why I like the front-engine Ferraris. That also means the GTO is the last year for those cars."

Before exemplary businessman Shirley became president of Microsoft, he admired the Italian marque. But he had his sights set on buying a Jaguar E-type, simply because he thought Ferraris were out of his price range. With the success of Microsoft came the success of Shirley's collection.

"My first car was a Sunbeam Alpine; it was a great car, except for the fins on the back. I drove it across the country several times." He bought the Alpine roadster after he moved from Boston. "I was living in Boston, and car insurance in Boston for someone under 25 years old was higher than it cost to take taxis everywhere. I'd rent a convertible every weekend, and it was still cheaper."

Today, Shirley has a collection of significant and important Ferraris, but he's most proud of his Alfa Romeo P3 grand prix car (tended by Enzo Ferrari's Scuderia) that whipped more powerful Auto Union cars in 1935 at the German Grand Prix. The more important the car in history, the better he likes it. And to house these machines, he's built an enormous metal building that gives each car enough space for people to wander and gaze at various distances to view the cars. It's not a museum—all of the cars run, and Shirley drives them in vintage racing events and at events he puts on by himself, renting race tracks such as Phoenix International Raceway for practice runs.

Shirley found the space to build his garage in the Pacific Northwest next to another building that was already being used by two car enthusiasts. He was leasing one floor of the building to store his cars and a burgeoning car model collection. He called the building his "clean room," where he kept his vintage race cars when they weren't at the mechanic's shop.

In the new garage building there are currently about 24 cars, spaced generously with a lot of room between them to walk and step back to gaze. One end of the building has a couple of offices with a mezzanine above them. The other end houses a workshop, separated by a system of folding glass doors. The workshop has a hydraulic lift, a full set of tools, parts storage, and a separate door to the outside. This area is used to keep the cars maintained, but at times it has been used for major work as well.

To keep the new building functioning, a full-time caretaker for the cars is necessary. Local enthusiast John Bennett, who had recently retired from a career at AT&T, took the job: "When we first started we thought we could do this three days a week. But we found there's no way we could get everything done even in five days a week." A bookkeeper occupies an office underneath the mezzanine four days a week.

The hardest part of keeping up the building, Bennett says, is keeping the dust off the cars. "It still collects a

Jon Shirley's collection of vintage race and sports cars is found in his immaculate garage, with plenty of space of walk around and admire the models.

Historical significance plays a dominant role in Shirley's selection. One example is the 1953 Ferrari 340/375 MM Competition Berlinetta seen in the foreground as No. 26. This storied Ferrari saw action in contests that included Le Mans, where it finished 5th overall, and Spa, where it took top honors. It was also raced in the Carrera Panamericana; in 2004, Shirley commissioned noted Ferrari specialist Butch Dennison to return the car to its 1953 Carrera Panamericana configuration and livery.

lot of dust, so we have to clean the floor every week." Fortunately part of the building design included two central vacuum systems, with hose outlets all along the walls. The mammoth air ducts are designed to change the air in the building three times every hour, mostly, says Bennett, to keep any exhaust from the cars from building up. "These fans will turn on if the system detects any emissions in here. They'll automatically turn on and flush everything out."

The main floor is simply set up to store cars, and all of the light maintenance is done on the other side of the folding glass wall. "That's where we do all of our oil and filter, brake fluid, antifreeze and other things," Bennett says.

Bennett does the maintenance on the cars himself, and also keeps track of which car needs what: "I inventory everything and keep records on the cars. I've got two maintenance manuals I use, and I've also got a pre-drive manual I use on all the cars." All of the cars are kept ready to drive at a moment's notice.

Bennett says they originally thought of putting air lines in the walls, but decided against the task because of its added complexity. The workshop area is well-designed, with built-in cabinets and two parts rooms, along with side-mounted lights. "This parts room is definitely not fancy. We've got all of our molds, race tires, spare tires, and race parts on the back side of that wall."

The shop is usually full of vintage race cars in various stages of preparation for racing season. Bennett manages the building and collection, but all the vintage preparation and all the Pebble Beach show cars are maintained at another shop. "This is the clean place," Bennett says. "We are constantly moving cars in and out of here. Every one of them gets driven. And so they spend time here. Usually Jon will call up and say bring these over to my house—he's only got a three-car garage on his house, and they're always filled up with cars."

About five times a year the facility hosts meetings for the Ferrari, Alfa Romeo, BMW, and other car clubs. "When the vintage races were in town, we once had a barbeque and luckily it didn't rain, and it was outside and the weather was great. We invited everyone, the corner workers, the other racers, and it was a big party," Bennett says. Shirley also has had charity events. Catered events get a tour and a talk about each car from Shirley.

Bennett mentions that the amount of wall space in the huge garage poses a problem for decoration: "The whole picture thing is kind of funny. We started out with a few pieces of art. And then Jon would bring three or four over once we had everything sorted and on the wall, and we would end up moving 22 pictures just to put one or two up."

Shirley is proud of his efforts to find clean, unrestored versions of cars he feels are significant. "I had to work to find this Austin Healey, and the XK120 with British Racing Green, and the '67 E-type that was not modified. It's hard to find one with miles on it that's still original and hasn't been rebuilt or restored.

"I also developed an interest in Alfas, after I saw the P3 racer. That is the best history of any car I have. It was driven by Nuvolari and it beat the Germans. They must have stood around and scratched their heads because they had faster cars, but Nuvolari still beat them."

Because Shirley drives several Ferraris on the racetrack and at events like the Mille Miglia in Italy, Bennett has gathered some insight about old Ferraris: "Ferraris can be on their death bed and they still run, they still go." This year Shirley drove an Alfa, however. "I just got back from the Mille Miglia and I had a '38 touring Alfa on that. It was a fantastic drive. I love driving the cars."

The quickest car that Shirley has driven is the '97 F310B Ferrari driven by Michael Schumacher. "The brakes are so much better than anything I'd ever experienced. Of course the acceleration is high, but the brakes are so good. When I first drove the car and I used the brakes, my glasses came forward and hit the inside of the helmet visor. I had to tape the glasses to keep them from sliding off of my head. The g forces are so high, you have to belt yourself in [very] tight.

"I just got back from driving it at Phoenix. If there's a hot Formula Atlantic and a competent driver and he's setting good times, you can go out in the Ferrari race car and match his times without trying very hard. That's without going into the corners quick enough to risk sliding off."

Another modern-day model in Shirley's stable is the

Among the modern-era gems in Shirley's collection is the first production Ford GT. He took delivery of the 2005 supercar in August 2004 (below).

first publicly available '05 Ford GT, the spiritual successor to the Ford GT40, the legendary Ferrari-beater of the late 1960. He took it to the racetrack as well. "When we took the car to Laguna to run it," Bennett recalls, "Ford flew one of their test drivers out, and we never got the car on the track because that was the day the car was recalled to fix the suspension. The car was grounded for four months, and then they had to come out here and spend 12 hours reinstalling everything. Each time, Ford sent one of their Roush mechanics out. Every one of those guys is a college graduate engineer; it was impressive. When we went to the track they sent out a pallet full of oil, all new rotors, pads, everything, and they never charged us for it. Great guys."

Although Shirley favors older Ferraris because they're classic front-engine designs, the new front-engine cars intrigue him. "The next car I'd like to drive would be the new series of front-engine Ferraris, the 599. I'd like to drive a Maranello. I've seen the 360/430; the 355 I love very much. I haven't driven a 250 SWB but I'd like to on the track."

Shirley learned to drive early. His uncle in Alabama let him drive the tractor around the farm. And Shirley's father ran a U.S. Marine Corps base in Puerto Rico, where, in junior high, he drove around the base. "My father told the Marines to look out for me and let him know if I was doing anything I shouldn't. I became a competent driver there."

Shirley credits his fantastic collection of Ferraris to the timing he chose to retire from Microsoft in 1990. "It was a great time to retire because the market for Ferraris had just fallen apart in 1989. It was a great time to buy cars. People would tell me that I was paying too much for a 166MM, for example, and they would say that's more than the car's worth. But I would tell them that I'm not buying the cars as investments, I'm buying them because I like them. In the long run, though, they did go way up in value."

He's shown some of his cars at the Pebble Beach Concours d'Elegance. "We have been to Pebble six times, and right after we finish a car there, we take it on a tour. Cars are meant to be driven. It's too bad there are some people who don't drive them."

One end of the garage building has offices with a mezzanine above them. Here visitors can see cars from above and scan the model and parts collection.

Shirley gets his hands dirty during restoration, too. "I completely restored an XK120, just like the one I have now." And if he's not doing the actual wrenching during a restoration, he's right in there with the mechanic. "When I have someone restore a car for me now, I do it with them. We pull the engine apart and look at the rods to figure out if they're stock or if the engine has been rebuilt. It's the only way to see what the car really looks like inside."

Shirley also started collecting models of his favorite cars around the time he retired. He estimates that he has about 500 now, enough that he had to store them with his real cars, because they wouldn't fit in his home. He designed the glass cases where the models are displayed, and he arranges them himself. "I don't spend as much time here in the garage as I'd like to, or in my garage at home. I came back from Italy with some models that were made in Belgium, some Alfa models, and I wanted to rearrange the display cases and add them to the cases," he recalls. "I spent a Saturday and Sunday alone here."

His tone indicates that life doesn't get any better than that.

Opposite: The shop, complete with hydraulic lift.

Kimi
SIEMENS
SAP

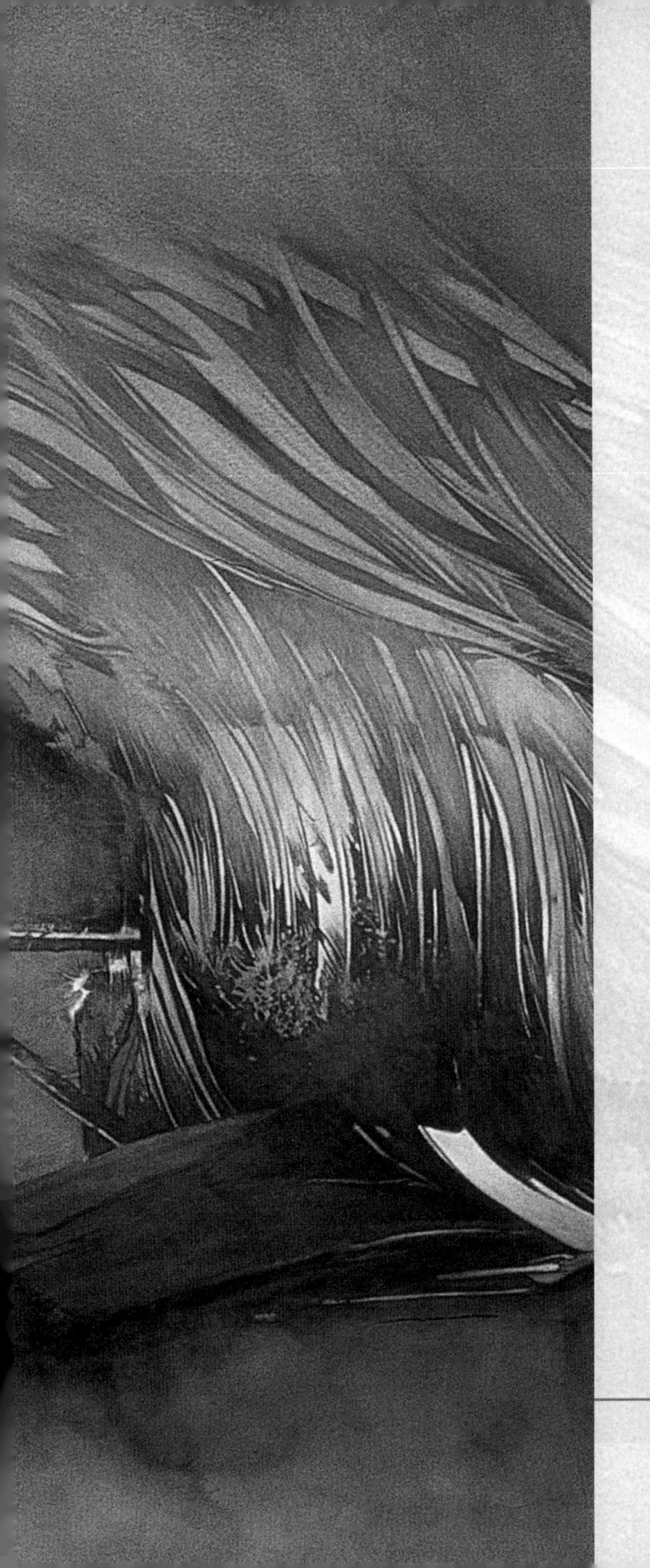

Motion Detector

Art Gallery with Niles Nakaoka

Niles Nakaoka's is a life in motion. His surfboard knifes the surface of Waikiki Beach's breakwater. His "day job" is associated with jet airliners. His mind often contemplates cornering F1 racers. Yet his countenance is as laid back as the Big Island itself, a quiet confidence that approaches the boldest forms of racing.

BY TRACY POWELL

Niles Nakaoka loves cars and all, but as a young man, he didn't read *Road & Track* to bone up on carburetion rates or compression ratios. Sometimes he didn't read the magazine at all. He just looked at the pictures. The photographs caught his attention, of course, but they did not capture his heart. The pictures Nakaoka hungered to see weren't the product of lenses and light but of palettes and paintbrushes.

He was looking for art, not eye candy. And when he found the art of painters like Hector Bergandi and William Motta, he did a lot more than look. He scrutinized, studied, dissected and adored.

"Those guys were gods to me," Nakaoka said, with a trace of awe in his lilting voice.

Nakaoka still looks up to those men and others, like his friend and mentor, Hector Cademartori. But he does so by choice, not necessity. He, too, is a bona fide, peer-approved practitioner of automotive art—quite an achievement for a self-taught, part-time painter and lifelong surfer dude who hasn't had an art class since high school.

Though his graceful, ebullient watercolors have won major awards at three of the last 10 Pebble Beach Concours d'Elegance, Nakaoka is like a batboy who suddenly finds himself playing center field for the Yankees. He can't believe he has made the major leagues.

But he most certainly has. Minor leaguers don't leave Pebble Beach with a Peter Helck Award, as Nakaoka did in 2002. Yet the 47-year-old Hawaiian was more excited about being counted in than singled out.

"The biggest honor of my career was being accepted into this association," Nakaoka said, referring to the exclusive Automotive Fine Arts Society.

Nakaoka was voted into the AFAS in 1995. He was delighted, of course, but didn't fully appreciate the distinction until after he was accepted.

"I didn't realize how difficult it is to get in," he said.

Actually, it's not—provided your artistic interpretation of speeding automobiles is sufficiently fresh, well executed and pleasing to the eye. Not just any eye, mind you, but the collectively keen and discriminating eye of one's peers. Nakaoka's paintings passed the test with truly flying colors.

Left: "Top of the World" 20 x 30 inches, 2005. Above: Niles Nakaoka in his Honolulu studio.

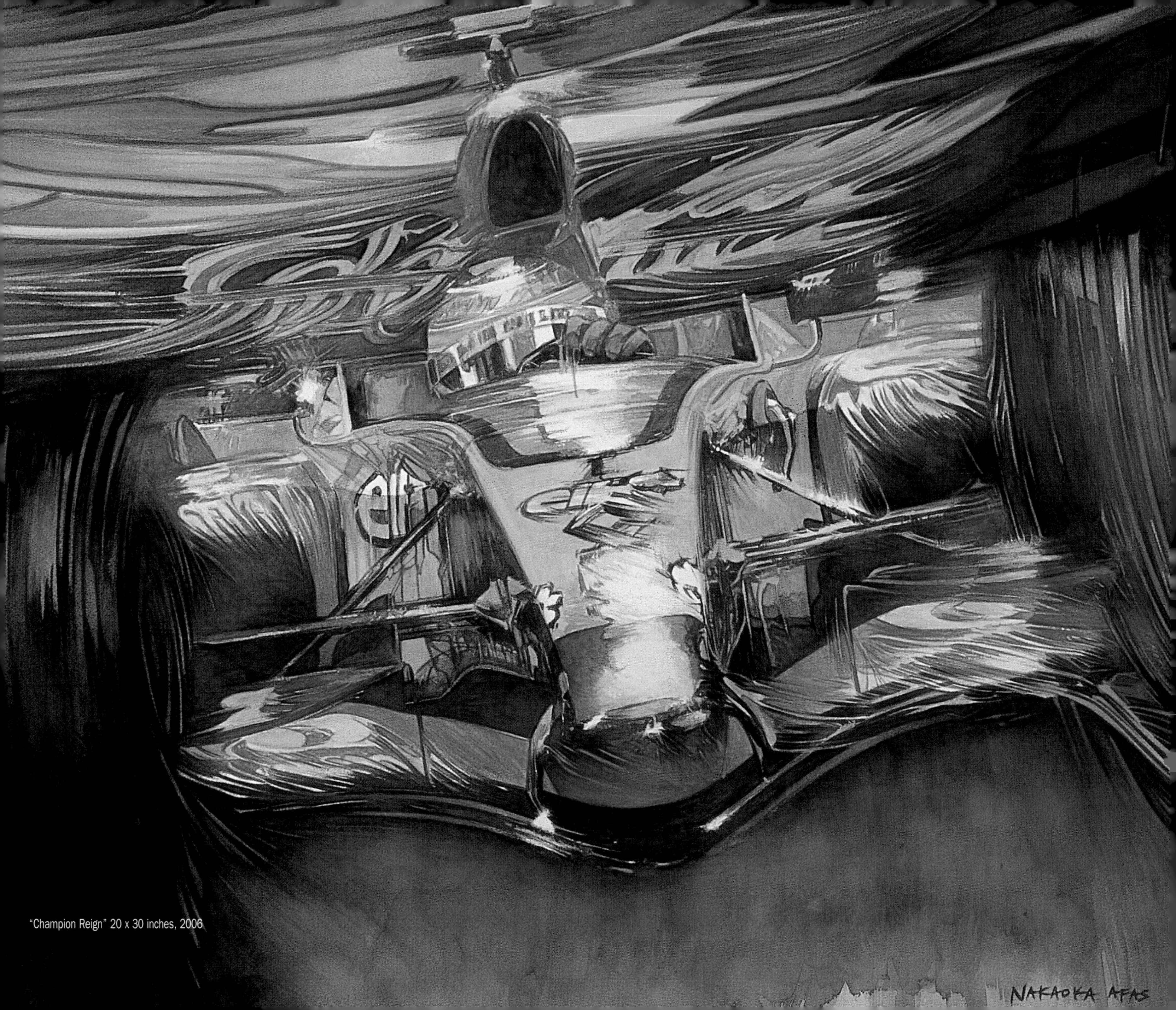

"Champion Reign" 20 x 30 inches, 2006

Capturing Moments in Motion

An exemplary expression of Nakaoka's distinctive style can be seen in "Letting It All Hang Out," an impressionistic rendering of Formula One driver Kimi Räikkönen in action.

"The styles of both (men) come together in an electric and energetic fashion that characterizes both of their talents," a *Road & Track* reviewer wrote.

The piece features the silver McLaren MP4-20 that the Flying Finn drove in 2002. But the viewer's eye focuses not on the car, which occupies less than a quarter of the painting, but on the dynamic swirls of color that frame an exaggerated burst of bright white. The composition suggests a racecar that is literally flying through a turn and off into the clouds.

"Letting it all Hang Out" is aptly titled. Nakaoka completed it in 2002, when after three decades at the easel, he finally quit thinking and started painting.

"I'm not forcing anything anymore," Nakaoka said. "Before, I'd be trying to make things work. The last three years or so, it's been really great. Things come a lot easier now. I've really hit my groove and come into my own, I guess."

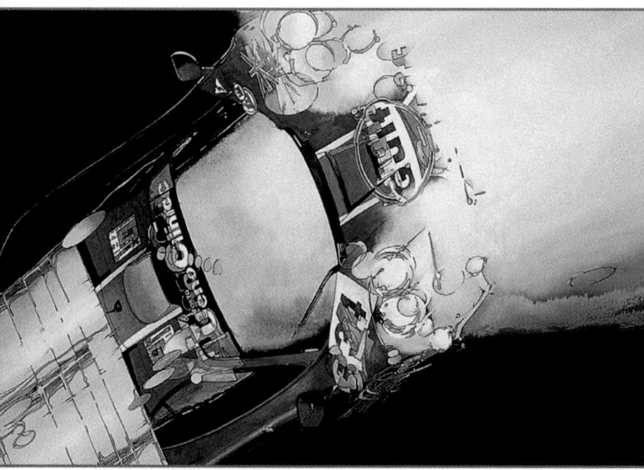

Above: "McLaren F1 Le Mans" 30 x 20 inches. Right: In "Flyin Gilles" Nakaoka depicts Gilles Villenueve racing in 1996. The painting was featured in *Racer* magazine in July of that year. 30 x 20 inches.

Above: "Flyin Lotus" 20 x 30 inches, 2003. Below: Painted in 2005, "Red Reign" 25 x 40 inches.

It used to be that Nakaoka only cut loose on his surfboard, slicing through the waves that crest in the shadow of the famous Diamond Head crater on Honolulu's Waikiki Beach.

"Growing up, I couldn't get enough of it," Nakaoka said. "Nowadays, I'm lucky if I can put in one or two days a week. I've really cut back a lot.

"A lot of it has to do with the crowds. It's getting dangerous out there. Plus, I'm getting older. I don't have that stoke anymore."

It is probably no coincidence that Nakaoka got less stoked about surfing as he got more stoked about painting.

"Before, at times I had to make myself get in the studio and do something. But I really look forward to painting now.

"Sometimes I get into such a groove that I can't leave it. I forget the time. I don't eat, I don't drink—nothing. If it gets too late, it kind of messes me up for the next day."

"I feel I've evolved and changed from the last few years, and become really comfortable and more developed in my own style."

Nakaoka works full-time as a ticket agent for Aloha Airlines (where his wife, Karen, is a flight attendant). He comes in at 4 a.m. and clocks at 12:30. It's a pretty swell shift for a guy who loves to surf, but less than ideal for an avid painter.

It's bad enough to have to cut short the creative binges that occasionally strike in the middle of the night. What is more unfortunate is that Nakaoka must spend so many productive waking hours behind a computer screen instead of an easel.

"I'd love to do this full-time," Nakaoka said. "But for me, painting is a side labor of love."

Nakaoka sold his first painting as a teenager, an abstract done in colorful acrylics. He made a down payment on a surfboard with the $50 he earned. His work commands substantially more than that now—he

Labatt
12
12

sells prints, artists proofs and unframed originals on his website, nilesnakaoka.com—but painting remains an avocation instead of a vocation. In 2003, he became a contributing artist with *Road & Track*, a lifetime dream come true.

Pebble Beach is the only show he does all year, which is why he still feels like more like a guest than a host at the grand annual party of his peers.

"I look around and think, 'Wow! I'm lucky just to be associated with these guys,'" he said. "Every August after Pebble Beach, I'm so stoked to get home and paint."

Nakaoka might always feel that way—because he always has.

Nakaoka's father, Hijoki, was a sheet metal worker. His mother, Beatrice, was a bookkeeper. There was no family tradition of unusual artistic talent, so little Niles and his preternatural knack for drawing were a pleasant surprise.

By fifth grade, Niles considered himself a pretty fair artist. But when he changed schools, he met an even more precocious lad named Wayne Fujiki.

One can see the influence of swirling surf in "Bending the T" (opposite). Above: From 1996, "Senna JPS/Lotus" 30 x 40 inches. Below: "Indyman/In Demand" 18 x 20 inches.

"I looked at his stuff and thought, 'Man, I'm nothing!'" Nakaoka said.

The boys struck up a friendly competition that lasted into high school. Both aspired to be commercial artists, but it didn't work out for either. Fujiki eventually gave up art as a serious pursuit.

Nakaoka did anything but. The arc of his career climbs higher all the time.

Over the past five years, Nakaoka has won the Peter Helck Award, his second Athena Award of Excellence and appeared numerous times in *Road & Track*, *Racer*, *Cavallino*, *Forza* and other automotive publications. He also is earning more commissions from patrons who appreciate his vibrant style and improvisational approach to composition.

Watercolors dry fast, clean easily and produce a unique brilliance and texture that Nakaoka prizes. But what he loves most about the medium is its flexibility. Watercolors permit Nakaoka to reinvent his paintings on the fly.

Above: "End of 9" 20 x 30 inches. Opposite: "M Schumacher" 30 x 40.

"I tell people that even I don't know exactly how my paintings will turn out," he said. "I do sketches, of course, but the actual painting usually takes me off in a different direction. As long as I get the essence of what people are looking for, they are satisfied with that."

So is Nakaoka, who feels more compelled to express himself than enrich himself.

In the recent past, commissions came from two women who wanted to surprise their husbands with paintings of their favorite cars—a 1932 Ford street rod for one, a Ferrari 250 GTO for the other. The ladies paid well, but a corporate order from Ford or Ferrari would, of course, have paid more. Perhaps the suits would have given Nakaoka free reign as well. With these women, however, there was no doubt. Nakaoka could let it all hang out.

"It was great," he said. "She just sent me some pictures and said, 'Do whatever you want.' Talk about a dream commission!"

His most recent commission also offered freedom of expression. A man from Texas found Nakaoka through his Web site, and a series of e-mails later the job was his. The client sent images and told Nakaoka to use any image with only one caveat: make sure the new rims and tires are included.

"I approach each painting with an image of what I want it to look like," Nakaoka said. "But it always turns out different at the end. I try to communicate not only motion, but emotion as well, and what you might imagine seeing."

Influencing his efforts are his environs and his occasional surfing pastime. The colorful, tropical flora – and people and art – hold a powerful sway over Nakaoka and his brush strokes, especially the colors. When he's on the water with board underfoot, his eyes capture the lights, darks, and colors cool and hot, "all swirling and bending together."

Also significant was a recent trip to Japan.

"My trip to Japan inspired me to look and view things in a different way," he said. "It's hard to say exactly what it is. I really enjoyed the food, and the culture. They appear to be so effective in what they do, I came away with a new release on the way to do things. I'll try to be more efficient in my art and life." AQ

Awards and Accomplishments

1995 becoming an AFAS member, which is "still the highlight of my art career."

1996 AFAS Athena Award of Excellence at Pebble Beach

2002 Peter Helck Award at Pebble Beach

2004 AFAS Athena Award of Excellence at Pebble Beach

AOKA AFAS

The Ascent

OF AUBURN

BY GRIFFITH BORGESON

When E.L. Cord became vice president and sales manager of the Auburn Automobile Co. in 1924, there were roughly 700 outdated Auburns in stock. But E.L., who provided the struggling company with ideas for interim salvation tactics, saw opportunity where others saw ruin. The young upstart would go on to take over Auburn and, after creating the new Cord line and acquiring Duesenberg among several other firms, lead the company to new heights. Most telling of E.L.'s meteoric rise in automotive lore is the evolution of the Auburn.

We do not know what the real terms of E.L. Cord's initial employment with the Auburn Automobile Company was. *Time* for Jan. 18, 1932, said that he had asked for no salary – just 20 percent of the hoped-for profits, plus the right to buy Auburn $25 par common stock for $20 a share. The *Philadelphia Record* said that his "one stipulation was that he would work without salary, providing he was allowed an opportunity to buy control, if he put the company back on its feet, at a price which would let the bankers out with a profit." Another source mentioned that he demanded absolute authority, with no interference from the board.

Above: E.L. Cord at an NACC directors' meeting in July 1930. Below: In 1925, body-to-chassis assembly (left) and the finishing room for wood and fabric bodies (right) at the Auburn Automobile Co. factory, Auburn, Ind.

Sales manager Harold Ames said, "They wanted to give him a salary. I don't know what it was, but it probably was something like $15,000 or $20,000 a year. But he wanted $10,000 a year and 25 percent of the profits. The directors really fought against his terms, but he finally convinced them that he was the man to do the job. He had to sell that one."

Cord demonstrated that existing Auburn models cost around $200 more than the nearest competitor. The line had to be replaced. He proposed the ELC SM for a start, convinced them of its potential price competitiveness and of its consumer appeal. He demonstrated to them how the first production run of 100 new cars could be swung with no cash outlay. Those Eskimos loved the icebox he showed them, and they were right.

Most sources agree that there were about 700 Auburn models languishing in inventory upon Cord's arrival. Sources also say that Cord had parts for about 1,500 cars, for which he had to buy engines. According to Ames, it was in connection with the liq-

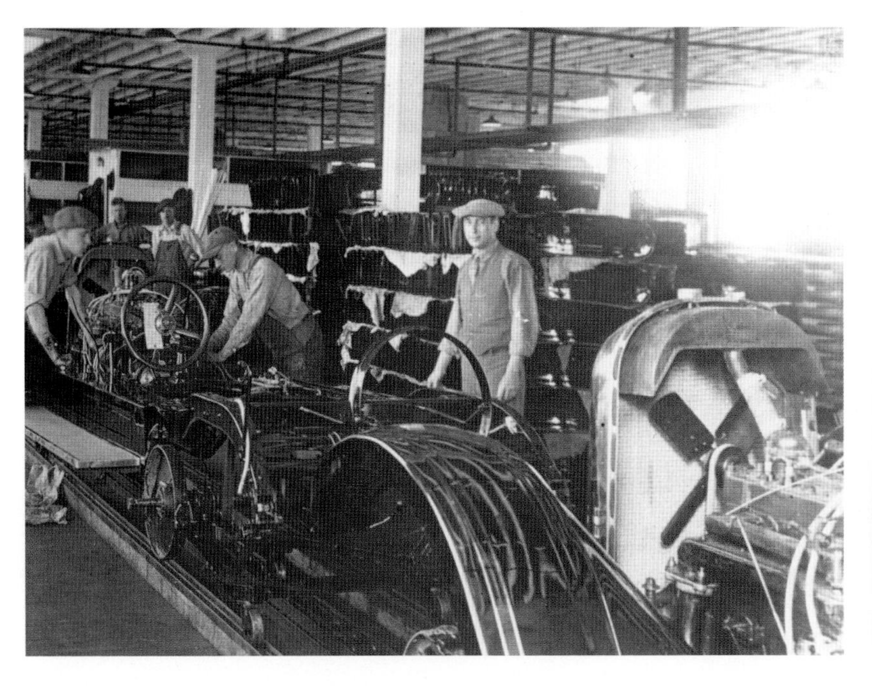

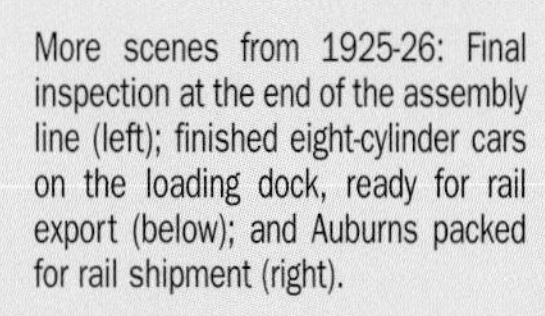

More scenes from 1925-26: Final inspection at the end of the assembly line (left); finished eight-cylinder cars on the loading dock, ready for rail export (below); and Auburns packed for rail shipment (right).

uidation of this old stock that Cord began doing business with engine-manufacturer Lycoming, which must have let itself be talked into making a better deal than Continental would. As for the exotic Weidely engine, it was very expensive, and Cord washed his hands of it.

According to the legend, he tarted up the existing stock with eye-grabbing paint jobs and a smattering of nickel plate and managed thus to sell the unsellable. Perhaps he did this with some of the cars. He dumped others in wholesale lots; there are near-contemporary reports of his making a $60,000 sale to a single large dealer in Brooklyn. But he disposed of a great many of them in conventional manner and in their "as is" state, just through revitalizing company relations with a broken-down and demoralized dealer organization that had been aimlessly adrift. This is demonstrated in two contemporary documents. One is a full-page ad in *The Chicago Tribune* for Sept. 21, 1924, another is a long article in *The Los Angeles Examiner* for Oct. 26; there had to have been many others. While not neglecting the habitual line of sixes, this publicity serves to introduce a new line of straight eights, the marque's big news for 1925. The car pictured is a type that had been in production since 1921; clearly, it was merely a case

of a new engine being made optionally available. It was a hulking 3.5 x 4.5 inch, 346 cid L-head Lycoming which, among other refinements, boasted a crankshaft vibration dampener. According to researcher Randy Ema, Auburn paid about $140 for this engine, as opposed to around $255 for the Weidely six.

Another document of real historical importance is a catalog – typically undated – for the new Auburn "8-In-Line," and thus from late 1924. Three body styles are shown, all of them looking a big lower, thanks to balloon tires on what probably are smaller disc wheels, and probably also due to some modification of the springs. All that is said about color is that fenders and flashing are black. One style is the old-fashioned standard Tourer and the other is the old razor-edge, boxy Sedan. Interestingly enough, the panels of this one body style are of aluminum. It looks as high as it ever did. Again, fenders and flashing are finished in black, while for the rest of the body the customer could choose between blue and maroon, period.

Examples of Auburn styling of the early '20s: The 1923 Auburn Beauty Six (above) and the 1924 Auburn "California Top" 6-43 tourer (below).

Concerning the third member of the line, the reader is told that "Style and distinction predominate in every line of the new Auburn 8-In-Line English Coach," the "European design" of which is stressed. It is a four-door, seven-window sedan, having a markedly lower top than its sisters. The top projects ahead of the vertical windshield, forming a visor. Unlike the thin slab of the Sedan top, this one is thick and curved in section and its sides and rear are amply radiussed. The shape of the top is a step in the direction of the ELC SM but lacks its finesse. The only element that might have been lifted from the historic rendering is a very wide band at the belt-line, bounded by slender molding beads above and below and lending itself to use as an area for playing with color contrasts. But this also was a feature of earlier Auburn models. As for color, you could have anything you wanted as long as it was what the catalog calls "A beautiful two-tone gray lacquer finish with moldings in black."

So here we have the disposition of an unknown

portion of the old stock through the usual dealer-retail channels. The straight-8 engine was all the rage, and if you couldn't afford a Model A Duesenberg or a Packard, here was your big chance, and at a moderate price. Although 1924 ended with claimed production of 2,400 cars, sales of 2,601, and gross receipts of $3,469,472, the bottom line still showed a deficit of $69,830 ... after Cord had paid the company's debts. Auburn's Ralph Bard could feel satisfied with his choice of savior.

Auburn's Turnaround Guy

Cord had another year-end deadline to meet: the eve of the opening of the New York Automobile Show, on Jan. 1, 1925. This did not give him much time in which to come up with a really all-new car, especially when there was little or no capital to work with. He traveled from one parts supplier to the next, selling his ideas, winning confidence, getting rock-bottom prices and the easiest possible credit. As for the translation of his personal design into a product that was technically sound, Cord depended upon the considerable competence of Auburn chief engineer James M. Crawford who, incidentally, also seems to have been responsible for the firm's body design and engineering. As for the execution of Cord's body design, in the fall of 1924 he persuaded the Central Manufacturing Co. of Connersville, Ind., to give him a bargain price and bargain credit on a run of 100 units. The Connersville company was eager to deal, the state's entire, once-flourishing automotive industry having been pushed to the wall by Detroit.

While the new model was being made ready for production, a couple of samples were completed in time for display at the New York show. No one in the little group of Auburn men who accompanied the cars to the world's most important automotive marketplace felt anything but knots in his stomach that New Year's Eve. Only the morrow would tell whether Cord's bet had been a good one or was a failure.

The verdict of the dealers – the primary customers – and of the public at the show was an enthusiastic endorsement of Cord's ideas. At the end of 1925, Auburn's sales totaled $7,746,907, wildly in excess of anything the company ever had known. With the memory of last year's almost $70,000 deficit all too fresh, there was a cash surplus of $655,432 with which to face the future.

Clearing out the last of the old stock had made its small contribution. One of Cord's devices for achieving this recuperation of revenue from outdated inventory was to introduce a four-cylinder model, fitting this Lycoming engine to the existing six-cylinder chassis. With a displacement of just 206 not-very-potent cubic inches, its performance was dull, but this was offset by fuel economy, along with a low price. Those who sought greater smoothness and a bit more go could have the same car with the slightly more powerful 196 cid Continental six. But the car that did the job and laid the foundation for the coming Auburn success story was Cord's own 1925 in-line eight.

This new model was not the ELC SM but, rather, a hybrid between it and the English Coach of the late 1924 catalog. Both it and the coach had seven windows, the same ungraceful crown fenders, a similarly rounded top, which they dared to call "streamlined," and the wide belt-line treatment. But the new car had the ELC SM's continuation of the lower belt-line molding or beading forward to the radiator filler neck. In place of the flat – in all senses – traditional Auburn radiator, that of the new car frankly took its inspiration from the rather elegant radiator of the Model A Duesenberg, which the latter shared with Duesenberg racing cars. It put a good deal of charisma where, up to then, the stuff had been totally lacking. The logically bounded areas now were available to be used for an infinity of color

The 1927 Model 8-88, a derivative of E.L. Cord's SM Coupe, has a Central-built body and a three-tone paint job that was typical of this model line. It is equipped with a windshield of Brewster design, a Lycoming straight-8, Columbia axles and Indiana Lamp headlights and taillights.

In August 1927, Eddie Miller and Wade Morton (left, behind wheel) headed a team of four Auburns that attacked stock-car endurance records on the Atlantic City board speedway. The 8-88 sports sedan covered 15,000 miles at an average 62 mph.

combinations: fenders and flashing; the body sides and top; and the belt area, which flowed over the top of the hood forming a graceful, pointed prow.

In place of the English Coach's vertical, evenly spaced louvers, the new car had four groups of four louvers on each side of the hood, and they sloped forward, giving a feeling of forward-straining movement. In place of the original eight's disc wheels, six-spoke wheels of pressed steel were offered as optional equipment. They had the look of artillery wheels, must have cost far less and, if not handsome at least were unusual. And in place of the former car's vertical windshield, the new one had one of the stylish, non-glare Brewster type, as foreseen in the ELC SM rendering. Although only a model year separated the new car from the '24 Auburn sedan, it was a decade ahead in styling. It had a look of solidity fused with grace. It was not beautiful, in the breathtaking sense of what was to come, but no one could say that it was lacking in good taste, nor that its elegance was more or less than was suited to its introductory price of $2,350. Wonder of wonders, it was eight inches lower than the '24. It catapulted the marque's images from a has-been in high-button shoes to the spearhead of the avant-garde.

The all-new, long, 130-inch wheelbase Auburn chassis was fully worthy of its coachwork. It did not indulge in novelties that deviated from the best conservative American practice. The frame was extremely substantial, the semi-elliptic leaf springs long and supple, and the system of four-wheel internal-expanding brakes was equipped with an automatic equalizing device. An early 1929 brochure states that "this car was a pioneer in the Straight Eight field – only three others had Straight Eights then." For all practical purposes, the 276 cid, 4525 cc Lycoming powerplant was not inferior to, say, Packard practice. It was well designed and well made. Its five main-bearing crankshaft, fitted with Lanchester vibration dampener, turned at a maximum of about 2,500 rpm in '25-'26 tune and, with proper care, the engine would run "forever." It used oil – about a quart every 400 miles – but that was par for the course in those days. A Swap inlet manifold helped to hold the big car's fuel consumption to a claimed 15 mpg average.

What began life as the Auburn Eight-In-Line became the 8-88 in 1926. *Autocar* for that Feb., 19 contains a rudimentary road test report of a specimen of this model, in which the maker's fuel-consumption claims were confirmed. Top speeds were found to be 25 mph in low, 43 in second, and 62 in high. This sounds slow and one is tempted to favor the factory claim of "2 to 68 mph in top gear." The test sedan weighed 3,696 pounds, pulled 4.63 final-drive gears, moved from 10 to 30 mph in 12.6 seconds in top gear and in five seconds in second.

Adding to the Line

It was presumably at the New York show in January 1926 that other body styles were added to the line, nearly all of them having E.L'.s prow hood treatment. There was a snappy roadster, with a Kissel-style top and the same advanced wind wings that went back to the Auburn sports tourer. There was an attractive coupe, with a Brewster-type windshield. And there was the brougham: the realization, in metal, of the ELC SM in the rendering that had helped sell the bankers. It was a very handsome car, although when it was equipped with the 6-66 engine the hood molding was a horizontal continuation of the belt-line lower head. The curved hood molding of the 8-88 was conspicuously absent from this model. Randy Ema reports that '25 and '26 6-66 models were known to exist with curved moldings. Through 1928, cars were available on special order, as for police use, with the more sober and severe straight molding. No phaeton seems to have been offered, perhaps because of another sensational idea on which Cord was working.

The existing body styles underwent only slight change in 1927, and the brougham was renamed the sports sedan. Cord added stock-car racing to his techniques of sales promotion and for the first time began citing performance figures in his advertising. The 276 cid 8-88 roadster was said to have a range in top gear of from 3 to 80 mph; top speed of the 196 cid 6-66 was given as 68 and that of the 226 cid 8-87 as 75 mph. A milestone was reached that summer, with the introduction of Auburn's Coupe Cabriolet, on the 8-87 chassis. It was one of the industry's first series-built convertible coupes – that is, having roll-up windows, as opposed to the roadster's side curtains. It was a very smart piece of design, a real breakthrough, and the prestige of the marque made another great leap forward and upward.

A shock of at least equal power hit the motoring public in January 1928, with the unveiling of the immortal Auburn Speedster, based on the 8-115 chassis, and priced at $1,895. Theoretically, it was a pure byproduct of the stock-car racing program and was Auburn's answer to Stutz's boattail, design to thwart the ability of other cars to get a free tow in the low-pressure area created in the wake of a speeding vehicle. The speedster's body was a much finer piece of design that that of the Stutz, and "rakish" is what it was. The lines of the hood louvers, doors, golf-club doors, and of the stern of the boattail all were raked backward at an angle of about 25 degrees. The windshield was sloped even more steeply, and the car's profile "read" smooth, flowing speed even when standing still. The characteristic "prow" hood molding of course was there, adding a touch of perfection to the marine allusion. The speedster was fitted with Dayton wire wheels and wing (knock-off) hub caps. Ten-spoke wooden artillery wheels were standard on all other models but the Daytons became optionally available throughout the line, bringing with them a highly racy effect. No other American make offered knock-off hubs and this styling coup was image-making dynamite, bringing Auburn that much closer to Rudge-wheeled European aristocrats and to American thoroughbreds of the speedways.

1929 Model 8-90. During the 1928-30 model years, speedsters were offered in two series: the big eight, including 115, 120 and 125 models, and small eights, including 88, 8-90 and 8-95 models. Fifty 8-90 models were built.

The hood louvers of all models, which had leaned forward in the past, now followed the example of the speedster, the new and super-sexy standard-bearer of the line. Among other marks of distinction, the speedster boasted 13-inch diameter headlights, the largest in the U.S. production-car field. These, too, were to be adopted by the rest of the Auburn line.

In 1929 the 299 cid engine of the 8-115 was equipped with improved inlet manifolding and dual-throat carburetion that enabled it to develop a claimed 125 bhp on non-premium fuel. This engine powered the

1928 Model 8-88 Sport Sedan. In 1928, Auburn introduced a series of three Lycoming-engined cars: a six-cylinder 6-76; a small eight; and a big eight called the 8-115. Built by Central Manufacturing, the 8-88 Sport Sedan shown here has wooden wheels, rear-mounted spare, three-speed non-synchromesh transmission and hydraulic brakes.

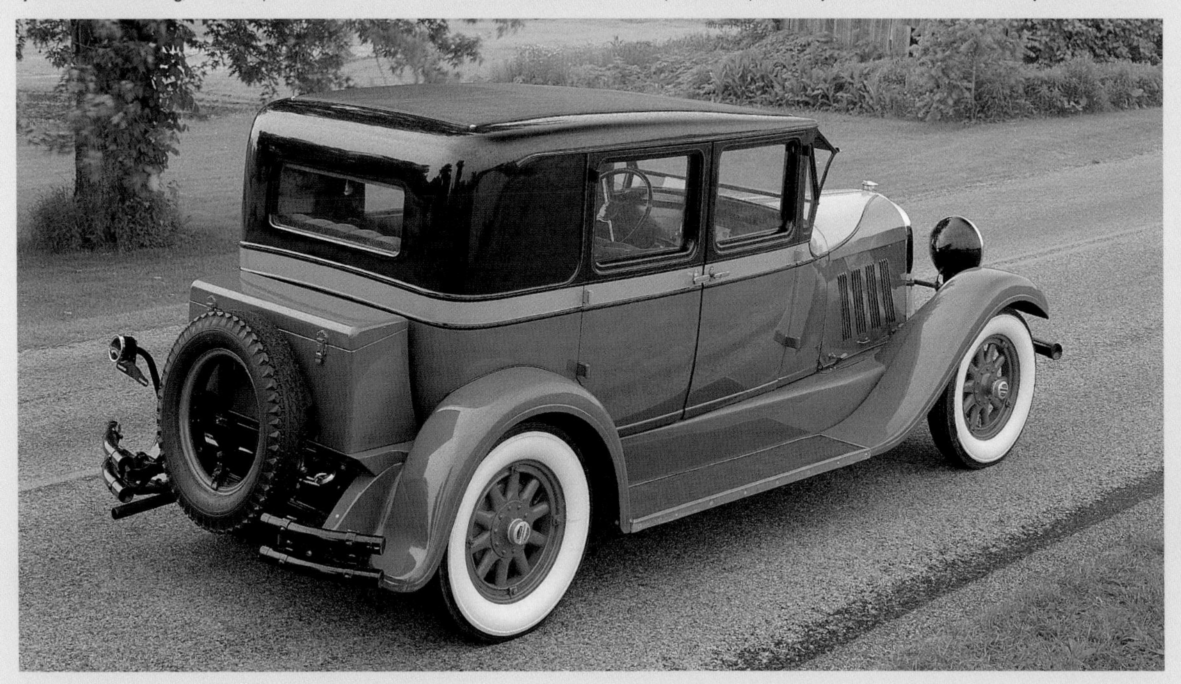

120, top-of-the-line chassis, one of the most powerful in the industry. The 120 models were notable for their use of chromium plate, then a novelty. And then in the summer came another spectacular milestone: also on the 120 chassis, introduction of the industry's first volume-produced convertible sedan, the Auburn "Phaeton Sedan, The Most Sensational Vehicle in the World." The prototype was built by Walter M. Murphy in 1927. Again, it harkened right back to the old ELC SM rendering of 1924. The basic design had been perfected in small ways over those five years into an ensemble of outstanding coherence and harmony. It had taken that long to achieve the effect that Cord had had in mind in the first place. A 1929 brochure stated:

"Design of the bodies of the Auburn models has been refined to make them a little more pleasing to the eye, and at the same time no radical changes have been made that would obsolete previous motor cars built during the last five years. This is a feature of great importance as it insures you that the car will not be obsolete when you decide to trade it in for a new one.

"Auburn continues to be the most individual and distinctive car in the industry by using the curved bead up over the hood, which is one of the most envied designs on any motor car, and has openly been copied in recent months by several makes of cars, some of them of custom design and the highest priced on the market."

A sales campaign was keyed to the theme "Continuity of Design Prevents Your Losing Money." It was implemented by ads that pictured this gradual but still marked evolution, as well as by motorcades that were staged all over the country, composed of specimens from each Auburn model year since 1924. Although it never was alluded to, all of the emphasis upon continuity pointed directly back to Cord's own 1924 design – the source of the basic, overall theme.

By early 1925, Cord had taken over as treasurer of the company, in addition to being its one vice president and its general manager. For these services and all the others that he rendered the company he received a salary of $1,000 per month. The list of officers and directors remained unchanged. With sales up 147 percent at the end of 1925 – 5,493 over 2,226 – he had proved himself to be a management messiah who had only begun to exercise his powers.

It was on Nov. 1 of that same year that the whole power structure changed. According to the plan that Cord had imposed, he had gotten the company out of debt, had bought out the bankers at a profit acceptable to them, and his takeover of the company was complete. The bankers picked up their chips and walked away and now the officers became R.S. Pruitt, secretary; L.B. Manning, treasurer; R.H. Faulkner, vice president; and E.L. Cord, president, at no increase in salary. He had turned 31 three months before. All this was irregular, original, and awfully sudden. The financial community and its media began to watch the new easy rider on their turf.

How had he done it? For one thing, he worked. He would arrive at the factory around 5:30 every weekday morning and go home around eight or nine at night. His son Charlie Cord remembered:

"He made money real fast. Once they got the old stock dolled up, then he went out on the road and sold them. My mother kept a sort of diary and I remember that, in '25 or '26, Dad spent 180 nights on trains. In a year's time. I was on a number of those trips, as a little kid. You'd get on the train in Fort Wayne and on the way to Saint Louis you'd stop two or three times – get

Within the confines of the company's new administration building, the upper-level engineering department. In the photo on the right, hovering over a drafting table with other key people, chief engineer Herb Snow is to the far left.

off and see the local dealer for an hour or a night, then get on the train and go on. He was out promoting the product that he was putting out. That was exactly how he had built up the Moon dealerships in Wisconsin."

With his colonization of Wisconsin for Moon, Cord did not have to buck the handicap of a loser's reputation. "No one had ever heard of an Auburn dealer who had made money," Cord used to say. He had to call on these bitter men, one by one, and sell his new plan, just as he had sold it to the bankers. It must have been a heroic job.

If dealers had suffered heavily as Auburn dug its way more deeply into failure, suppliers had no happier memories of experience with the marque. There were probably more of them than there were Auburn dealers, and they all had to be called on and, above all, sold. This was a new sort of activity for Cord, and he recalled having "worked harder on the people from whom we bought than on those to whom we sold." He apparently did an excellent job of it.

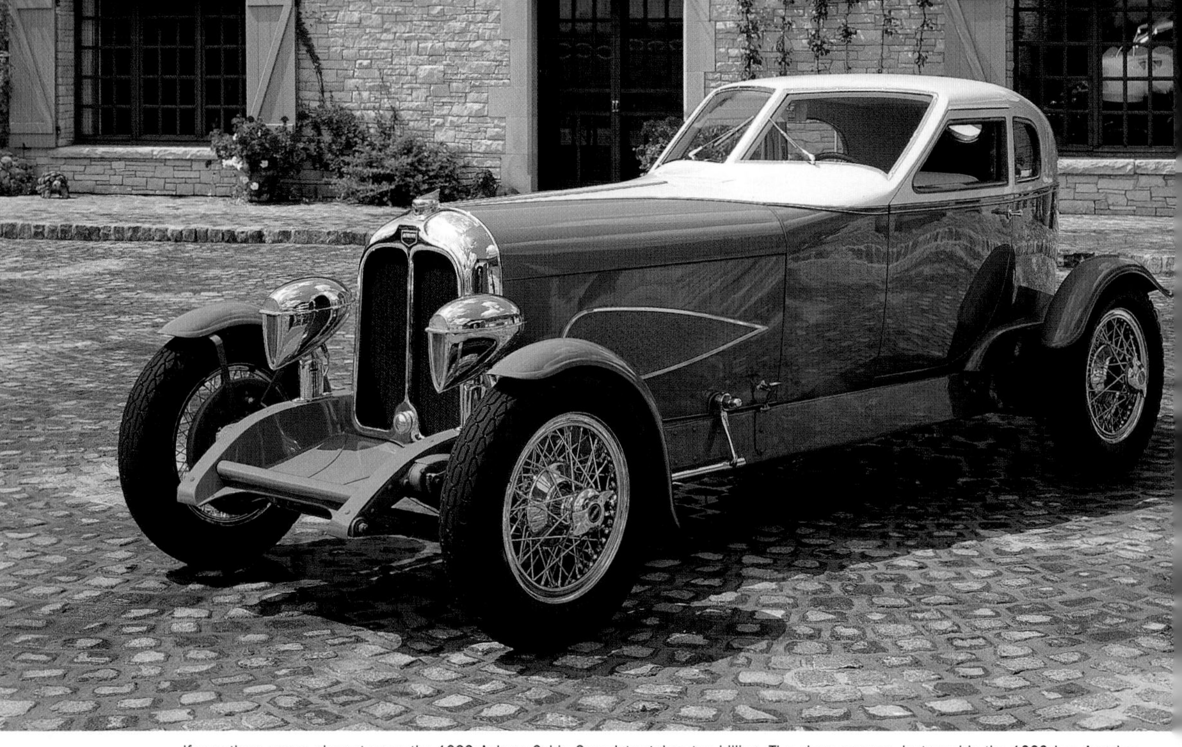

If ever there was a show-stopper, the 1929 Auburn Cabin Speedster takes top billing. The show car was destroyed in the 1929 Los Angeles Automobile Show fire. The radical lines and prescient engineering was brought back to life in this recreation (see *AQ* Vol. 25 No. 3).

Also new to him was running a good-sized manufacturing and sales organization. What had been esteemed as good business practice under the administration of the bankers seemed ridiculous to him. He tore out lint-picking, time-wasting systems that had satisfied the criteria of efficiency experts, got rid of tons of paperwork, and set up a new order of common sense.

He got rid of some human deadwood, but that was the least of the problem. Most of the demoralized personnel wanted nothing more than to have work to get their teeth into and, by God, he saw that they got it. With his enthusiasm and sense of going places, they seem to have eaten it up.

Cord had a philosophy of his own about hiring. He would not hire a man away from another employer for equal money or for more money. Nor would he hire a man for the going standard scale. For such employees, he said, there was just one day in the week: pay day. What he sought and chose were men and women whom he could so infuse with enthusiasm for what he wanted to build that they would work for less. It was not just that he was frugal – he chose those who were willing to make a moral and material investment in the enterprise, who would have a vital personal stake in it and who couldn't wait for the start of each new work day.

His technique, at the start, was to sell distinction in his products. He could not compete on grounds of performance or price, so he tried to compete by being different. Hence the English Coach, and it caught on during its brief lifespan at the beginning. He used the Coach as a lure to get people into showrooms and, every time he sold a couple of the things, he managed to palm off an obsolete sedan. This, along with simple department-store bargain-basement discounting, was part of his strategy for the clearing out of out-of-date stock, and for the very rapid liquidation of the company's indebtedness.

The year 1925 started out as a sellers' market, so that it was impossible to tell whether the new brougham was a hit on its own merits, or was just sharing the crest of an economic wave. By summer, the bubble had burst and price wars had begun. To be sure of retaining his competitive position, Cord was tempted to slash prices. Instead, he took the gamble of maintaining them unchanged, in order to see if it were not perhaps the attractiveness of the car itself that had made it seem to be not badly accepted by the public. This bet paid off. Auburn sales stayed up, and by late 1925 he knew, finally and for sure, than he had something of a hit on his hands.

These are just a few of the things that he did, more or less single-handedly, to make something out of Auburn in the early days. Calm and quietly profane though he may have been, he was a permanent firestorm of mental and physical energy.

Winning Financial Strategy

How did Cord do it financially? Cord believed in keeping a minimum of paper on file, but he probably had nothing to do with the massive destruction of Auburn company records that took place when, in 1937, he disposed of his manufacturing empire and the new owners immediately got out of the automotive business. Most of the archives went up in smoke, leaving little for the patient researcher to unearth. Happily, some highly significant information found its way into print at the time and is recoverable today.

For example, Michael Rosen's research in Spanish periodicals documents that as early as October 1925, Cord had a hard-driving export division in operation. A steady stream of full-page ads shows that he did not use the export market for dumping a product that was hard to sell at home. Foreign buyers were offered the latest, as soon as it became available, along with "complete stocks of replacement parts." No doubt a few oldies and moldies were palmed off in the heat of the action. In February 1927, the company had distributors in Amsterdam, Athens, Berlin, Brussels, Bucharest, Copenhagen, Hamburg, Lisbon, London, Oslo, Paris,

The basic body of the 8-90 Speedster ('29 model shown here) was created in 1927 for the Model X Duesenberg. Intended as a promotional model, the two-seater speedster appeared in such dramatic color combinations as yellow and black and also maroon and cream.

Prague, Riga, San Sebastian, Vienna and Zurich. The distributor in San Sebastian had agents in most important Spanish cities and it can be assumed that similar coverage existed in other countries. The Western Hemisphere received as much attention as did Europe. A constant selling theme was "The Greatest Value for the Least Cost," value including comfort and elegance. European old-timers with whom I have spoken remember the Auburns of the late '20s as having enjoyed the same class image as Cadillac, Lincoln and Packard. Starting out with 7.3 percent of sales to export markets in 1924, Cord built this sector up to 17.3 percent in '28, after which it settled down to between 11 and 12 percent – a comfortable figure – in '29 and '30.

Cord's acquisition of control of Auburn can be reconstructed as follows. The gentlemen habitually referred to as the bankers, who bought Auburn in 1919 for a round million dollars, issued 10,000 shares of $100 par-value preferred stock. This stock had preference as to the firm's assets and had the right to 7 percent annual dividends. The stock was to be "retired" at the rate of not less than $100,000 annually, until the total investment had been recuperated out of earnings by the financiers, the final deadline being Jan. 1, 1930. They would have loaned their money to the company, it would have been paid back, and they would own the company free and clear. In addition to their 7 percent and at least token salaries, the company was intended to produce surplus earnings after all indebtedness had been paid off. To guard against the possibility that a bad year might come along and the minimum $100,000 stock-retirement payment not be available, the company was caused to maintain a sinking fund, of no less than that amount and earmarked for that specific use. The stock itself, owned all or mainly by the financiers, was expected to appreciate in value. It was a good deal – a nice, conservative exercise in capital risk.

The plan was a flop almost from the start. After raking in a resassuring $439,236 in net earnings for 1920, these sank disastrously to $126,437 for '21, then on to a deficit of $12,220 for '22. The depression of 1920-21 had made its contribution to this careening chute, but there were other factors in operation. It was not that Auburn was not making good cars; it was not making competitive cars. In addition, it was not Auburn alone that was in dire straits, but Indiana's extensive automobile industry as a whole. Some authorities blame the State of Indiana's heavy taxation of industry for this result. Others say that the real cause was that the industry in Michigan was beginning to achieve national dominance, an outstanding reason for this being the far lower cost of transporting raw materials and products by water – the Great Lakes – than by rail. In the absence of an Errett Cord to show them how to fight against such odds, Hoosier manufacturers quietly died away.

At Auburn, the deficit increased nearly tenfold in '23. Almost certain bankruptcy seemed to lie not far ahead, along with the definitive loss of the bankers' remaining half-million dollars. When they tried to hire Cord, he probably laughed and told them something like: "Gentlemen, what I am offering to do is to perform a miracle by bringing your company back from the dead and by saving your investment. It will require half killing myself, and I will make that sort of effort for no one in the world but myself. So these are my conditions: in exchange for saving your investment, I want to be permitted to buy your failing company. And to save it I am going to have total, unhindered control, just as soon as it becomes apparent that my plan is working."

Alan Leamy (left) has his hand in several Auburn designs, and is well-known for his involvement with the Cord L-29. Above: 1929 Model 120 cabriolet, a big-eight-powered model with optional wire wheels, side mounts and trunk.

They seem to have gone along with him, to the letter. By some financial alchemy known to initiates of their calling, the outstanding $500,000 in preferred-stock indebtedness was retired. In its place the bankers substituted $600,000 worth of $1,000 debenture 6-percent gold notes, which they held. This obligation of the company was dated Nov. 1, 1925, and it had to be paid off, along with all interest, by that date in 1930. Each $1,000 note, when paid off, was convertible into 16-and-two-thirds shares of preferred stock, meaning that this stock had a real value of $60 per share; 10,000 shares existed, representing the $600,000 which, with interest, the bankers wished to get back out of Auburn. The situation was similar to selling a house on time, with the purchaser taking immediate occupancy. In effect, the bankers set up a loan for Cord as soon as he had proven his credibility, and he was given immediate occupancy of the property. At this point it was announced publicly that he had been "elevated to the presidency." Rather sportingly on the bankers' part, this loan was not secured by a mortgage on the company's physical assets. However, the company, meaning Cord, contracted "to maintain quick assets at 125 percent of current liabilities, including this issue," or loan. It was secured additionally by the deposition, with the trustee bank in the affair, of a quarter-million-dollar insurance policy on the life of hopeful savior E.L. Cord.

I trust that this is perfectly clear. It took a while to sort out.

Auburn's common stock also underwent considerable evolution at this same period. Back in 1919 the issuing of $750,000 worth of $25-par shares had been authorized and carried out. On the strength of the Cord management's swift success, authorization was obtained on Aug. 15, 1925, to increase the common issue to $1.5 million and, on Nov. 14, to double that again. At the end of 1925, $1,689,300 in Auburn common was outstanding, of which $1,310,700 was in the company's treasury. Cord had been pouring his personal capital into this stock from the moment he became established at Auburn, at a time when its market value was well below its $25 par. Large acquisitions at $3 and $4 have been mentioned in print. With the new issue, Auburn became listed on the Chicago Stock Exchange and quoted in the New York Curb Market.

Thanks to the new vitality with which Cord had infused company and product, Auburn common varied during 1925 between 31.75 and 56.50, a nice spread, leaving ample room for lots of profitable action, above all for the chief insider.

The first payment on the debenture loan — $100,000 – fell due on Nov. 1, 1926. That year, after paying $256,703 in common-stock dividends, the company had a cash surplus of $686,559. Of course there was no problem in making the payment on the loan. As a matter of fact, under Cord's management the company's working capital had increased from a nominal $967,962 in '24 to $3,829,989 in '25, to $5,840,348 in '26. Common stock now outstanding represented $2,122,220 at $25 par, and it sold during the year between 40.50 and 72.87. Ralph Bard, justly content with the astuteness of his vision and proud of his protégé, was brought back by Cord to the board of directors.

In 1927, sales climbed from $10,327,205 to $14,819,972 and cash surplus from $689,559 to $912,704. At the bankers' request, Cord agreed to maintain total current assets equal to 200 percent of liabilities and net current assets of at least twice the value of outstanding notes. There was not a day that his treasury did not contain millions in cash. Authorization was received to increase common stock from the former limit of $3 million (120,000 shares) to $12.5 million (500,000 shares at $25 par). As of June 22, 1927, the stock's par value was dropped, as outstanding shares were increased judiciously from 84,888 to 127,600. The market value of the stock varied between 69.00 and 123.50 during 1927.

In 1928, sales made another leap, from $14,819,972 to $16,451,133, in spite of a decline in unit volume and the fact that operating expenses went up by a full $2 million. Still, the company finished the year with a surplus of $886,243. Total common shares issued had been held to a modest 141,450. They sold during the year for between 78.00 and 141.25.

Opposite: Designed by Al Leamy, this 1931 Model 9-98A Speedster belonged to a lineup that was offered only with the eight-cylinder GU Series Lycoming engine. This page: Two views of Leamy's wooden mockup proposal for the 1931 Auburn. Many of the lines were retained, but the radiator shell was rejected.

In 1929, sales shot from 12,899 to 23,297 units – a gain of 80 percent. Sales revenue soared to an undreamed-of $37,551,442 – up 128 percent. Cash surplus increased 151 percent, to $2,226,587. Missing from financial reports was any mention of the old debentures, obviously liquidated and retired a year ahead of schedule. The company redeemed the last of the premium stock from the bankers and now Cord was fully its master, and a multi-millionaire. His once-mortgaged life-insurance policy even had acquired a cash value of $33,696. A few more shares of common stock were issued, bringing the total outstanding to 169,689.

Auburn at last became listed on the New York Stock Exchange, where it became one of the all-time glamour issues, oscillating insanely between $120 and $514 per share during the course of the year. Cord, aged 35, was a national celebrity and hero – distinctions that altered his calm, cool manner not at all. The press, general as well as automotive, was enchanted by this almost boyish fulfillment of the American Dream. AQ

Capturing an *Era*

The Roy Stryker Collection

THE STANDARD OIL (NEW JERSEY) PROJECT 1943-1950

It was a time like no other. At the beginning of the Standard Oil Project in 1943, America was immersed in a world war on two fronts that consumed manpower and material resources at an astronomical rate. Passenger car production had been suspended in favor of war-related manufacturing. That, coupled with gasoline rationing and rubber shortages, found traffic volume on the nation's highways to be less than half that of prewar years. At its conclusion, however, interstate highway construction was in full swing and an enormous appetite for new automobiles kept all factories humming.

The Standard Oil Project came into existence in hopes of creating a bank of photography that would become a PR tool to assist the company with their quest to portray the corporate giant in a more positive light. There were opinions to mold, sway and in some cases reverse to achieve their goals. To lead the effort, they called on Roy Stryker, who had just finished such a project of a similar magnitude for the Farm Services Administration during the early years of Franklin D. Roosevelt's administration. The resultant Stryker Collection remains one of great photographic treasures of the era.

BY GERRY DURNELL

Washing the car, Wyoming (Edwin and Louise Rosskam, 1944).

The Stryker Creative Criteria...

... "Insatiable curiosity, the kind that can get to the core of an assignment, the kind that can comprehend what a truck driver, or a farmer, or a driller, or a housewife thinks and feels and translate those thoughts and feelings into pictures that can be similarly comprehended by anyone."

--Roy Stryker

Roy Stryker on location in Louisiana with documentary film makers Richard Leacock, and Robert Flaherty filming *Louisiana Story.*

Roy Emerson Stryker was born Nov. 5, 1893, in Great Bend, Kansas, and later migrated with his family to live in Colorado. He enjoyed growing up in the life of the cowboy, working with cattle on homestead land and in the winters taking a turn in the mines of Montrose, Colorado. In contrast, Stryker demonstrated an early affinity for reading, chemistry and the sciences. He tried college but weak eyes and lack of money proved discouraging.

The hard work of the range and the mines agreed with Stryker. His eyesight improved, and when the time came he enlisted in the U.S. Army as an infantry soldier during World War I. During his "hitch" he enjoyed the intellectual inspiration of some of his fellow soldiers and made plans to restart his quest for higher education. His school of choice was Columbia University in New York, but an adamant Army rule of their choice of discharge locations took him back to Fort Leavenworth, Kansas, delaying his plans.

During his freshman year in 1921 at Columbia, a friendship with economics professor Rexford Guy Tugwell later proved to be a turning point in his life.

Stryker family in Great Bend, Kansas in front of dormitory for local college in which the family lived and provided management.

Tugwell introduced Stryker to publishing through an involvement in a book project he was working on, and Stryker was named joint author for his contribution of illustrations for the book. Stryker had earlier demonstrated a knack for developing illustrations and visual aids for instructors' classes and bulletin board use, so he was delighted to be included.

Stryker was appointed Assistant in Economics at Columbia following the receipt of his bachelor's degree in economics in 1924. A variety of teaching positions followed. In 1932 his old friend and former instructor was asked by Raymond Moley, a neighbor and colleague at Columbia, to contribute ideas and talk about economics with then-governor of New York Franklin D. Roosevelt, who was considered a likely candidate for the presidency.

Just as John F. Kennedy had his cadre of "Whiz Kids" as a close advisory group, Roosevelt compiled his "Brain Trust," largely taken from Columbia. Three principal advisors emerged including Raymond Moley, Adolf Berle and Tugwell. Following a landslide election in 1932 and the administration transition in 1933, the New Deal was born and an "alphabet soup" of ideas and institutions such as WPA, AAA, FSA and RA took shape. Tugwell's former student was drawn to the nation's capitol and found work in the information division of the Agricultural Adjustment Administration (AAA).

By the end of 1935 the evolution of the "alphabet soup" had distilled Stryker's activity into the Resettlement Administration (RA). He had four talented photographers: Arthur Rothstein, Carl Mydans, Walker Evans and Dorthea Lang. Others would later join their efforts, which now focused on a photographic mission to complete a visual documentary of the American way of life in the 1930s. Reorganization in 1937 gave the little bureaucracy a new name as the Farm Security Administration (FSA). During the life of the organization, Stryker and his team were able to explain the problems of rural poverty and the impact of the Depression, which in turn led to legislative action and various programs that would ease the massive transition of America from a rural to an urban culture.

By 1950, the total cost of the project had surpassed $1 million and the photographers had produced 67,000 black-and-white images and at least 1,000 color transparencies.

During World War II, the photographic unit was incorporated into the Office of War Information and then disbanded in 1942, whereupon the holdings of the FSA's photographic unit were transferred to the Library of Congress. Stryker resigned from the FSA and went to work on a documentary project of similar scope for Standard Oil, which lasted from 1943 through 1950.

Roy Stryker and Carl Maas, in the public relations department of Standard Oil checking layouts and choices of photographs.

Major clients that followed included the Pittsburg Photographic Library and Jones & Laughlin Steel Corporation. Stryker was generous with his time doing consulting work and conducting seminars on photojournalism at the University of Missouri. He retired and returned to the West in 1960. He died in Grand Junction, Colorado, on Sept. 27, 1975. The complete Standard Oil collection now is housed at the special collections division of the Ekstrom Library at the University of Louisville in Louisville, Kentucky.

Although not a photographer himself, Stryker's mentoring provided insightful guidance and inspiration to the members of his team and, later, students of the craft. His methods had an enormous influence on the development of modern photojournalism and later became guidelines for photo-rich editorial content such as was utilized by *Life* and *Look* magazines.

Today, the Stryker legacy is principally recognized by his role as one of the great photographic archivists of the 20th century. Through the auspices and support of, first, the United States government and later the corporate giant Standard Oil, Stryker was able to amass two of the most significant photographic collections of the time featuring the works of some of the most renown and respected photographers in the history of the art.

In this day of smart, miniature cameras that automatically measure photographic light requirements, digital options and fast film, it's hard to imagine toting a 15-pound camera like the cumbersome 4-in x 5-in Speed Graphic with all the attendant equipment such as bulky flash units, power packs, exposure meter and film holders on assignment. In reflection, it makes the work of Roy Stryker and his team all the more remarkable.

Images of Standard Oil

Standard Oil was in trouble. Although they were the world's leading producer and distributor of petroleum products, public opinion held them in exceptionally low regard. New York's public relations maven Earl Newsom was called upon to rescue the struggling giant. He found that not only was the oil industry generally considered to be corrupt, but that Standard Oil was held even lower in surveyed opinion.

Part of the reason for the public's wartime rationale was the revelation of an earlier patents cartel formed in 1929 by Jersey Standard and Germany's I.G. Farben. When Standard Oil developed a new synthetic rubber called butyl it turned the process over to the German petro giant and refused to give it to the U.S. Navy. Given that the war in the Pacific had cut off 90 percent of the country's natural rubber supply, it was a rather sensitive issue at the time; so much so that then-Senator Harry Truman was moved to shout "Treason!" during congressional committee hearings. As *Time* magazine reported, "Standard was damned from hell to breakfast. But this week when the company finally got a chance to reply, its 'treason' turned out to be strictly of the dinner-table variety."

Still, the damage was done and the public perception remained.

One of Newsom's senior employees, Edward Stanley, who was familiar with Roy Stryker's previous archival work on the Farm Security Administration (FSA) project, suggested in mid-1943 that Standard Oil create a documentary photographic project that would follow the creative style of FSA's successful efforts.

On Oct. 4, 1943, Stryker agreed to join the company and the project idea became a six-year reality. The collection was developed and made available to magazines, newspapers, writers and artists at no charge. The only requirement was the use of a credit line in connection with the published photograph with attribution to Standard Oil Company (N.J.). In 1949 alone, approximately 50,000 prints were distributed for publication and exhibits; however, corporate budget trimming in 1950 brought the project to a close.

"To tell the story of oil from the jog on the seismographer's chart to the car, home or business of the user—and to tell it always with the accent of the man on the job: from scientist to roughneck, from pipeline rider to service station operator."

—project photographer's mission statement—

On an oil derrick, Oklahoma (Corsini, 1946).

Hands of a driller's helper, Kentucky (Corsini, 1944).

Burning Naptha tank, Louisiana (Webb, 1948).

Overalls drying, Texas (Corsini, 1946).

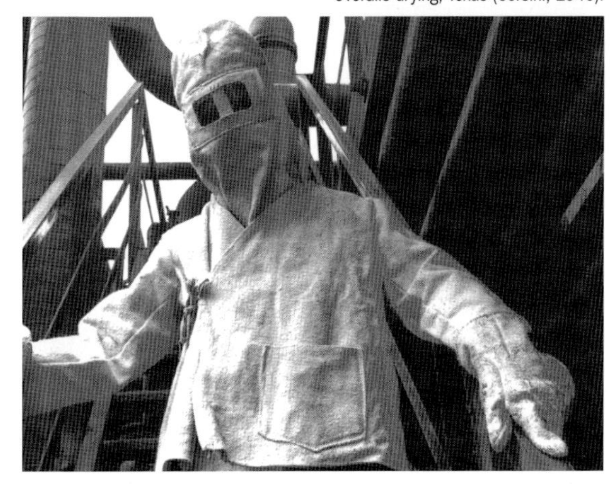

Asbestos safety suit, Texas (Rosskam, 1944).

Cleaning a drum, Pittsburgh (Bubley, 1944).

Truckdriver after a run, Ohio (Libsohn, 1945).

Refueling on the Pennsylvania Turnpike (Libsohn, 1945).

Mail delivery, North Dakota (Vachon, 1948).

Service station owner, Oklahoma, (Corsini, 1946).

Street scene, Oklahoma, (Corsini, 1946).

Early morning fog, Massachusetts, (Brooks, 1946)

Leaving the bus terminal, New York City (Bubley, 1947)

Postwar: The Good Years

With victory in Europe and the surrender of the Japanese in 1945, America shifted its economic attention from the requirements of war to the opportunities at home. Wartime restrictions on road building were lifted and the largest highway plan in history was undertaken by state highway departments across the nation. Returning GIs came home to unprecedented educational opportunities through the GI bill and VA loans made the dream of home ownership a reality within grasp.

Clover-leaf intersection, New Jersey (Rotkin, 1949)

Standard Oil (New Jersey) Project Photographers

Berenice Abbott
Charlotte Brooks
Esther Bubley
John Collier*
Harold Corsini
Arnold Eagle
Morris Engel
Elliott Erwitt
Russell Lee*
Sol Libsohn
Lisette Model
Martha McMillan Roberts
Gordon Parks*
Edwin* & Louise Rosskam
Charles Rotkin
John Vachon*
Todd Webb
*(also worked on FSA)

Soldier on furlough, North Carolina (Libsohn, 1944)

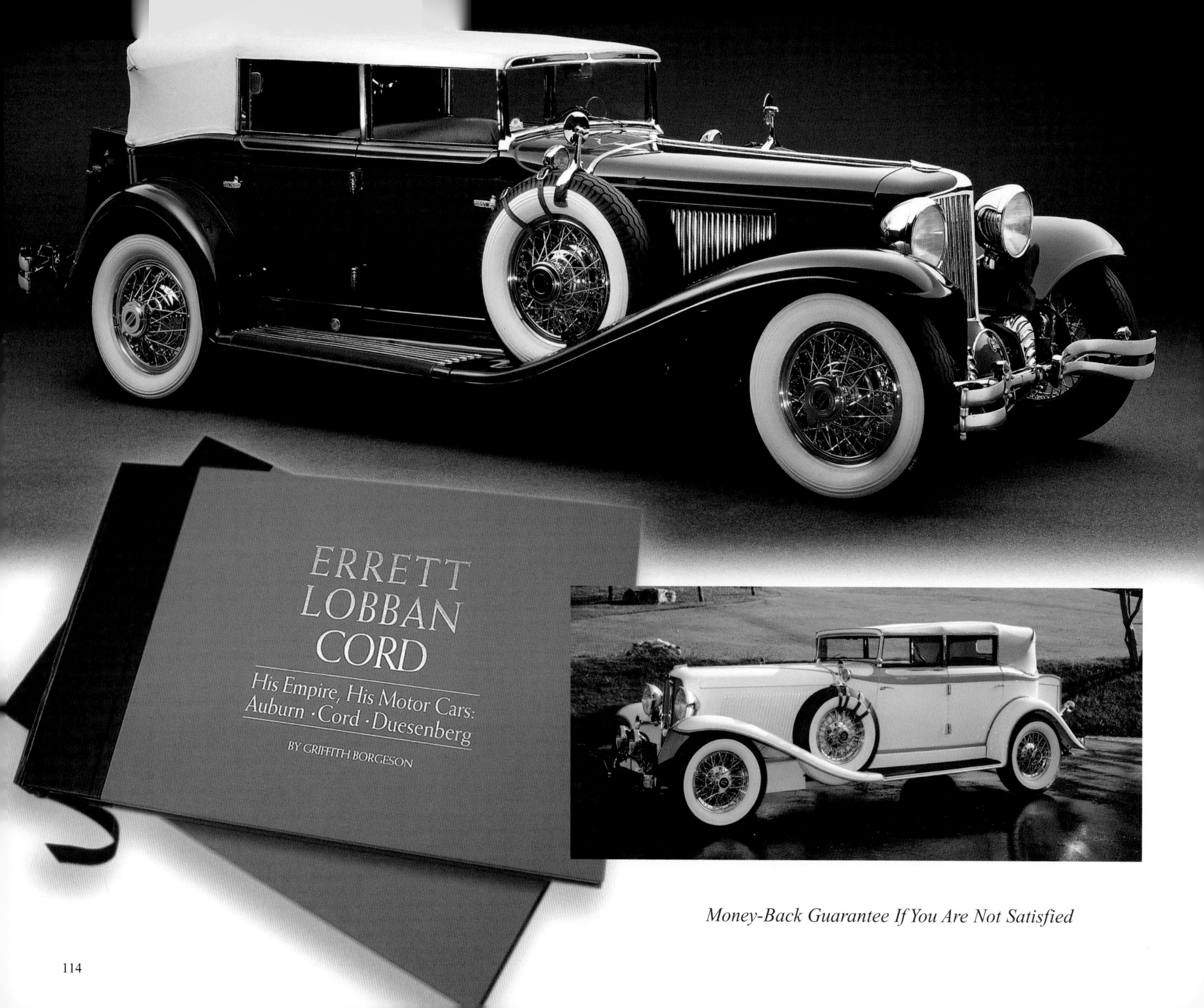
ERRETT
LOBBAN
CORD
His Empire, His Motor Cars:
Auburn · Cord · Duesenberg
BY GRIFFITH BORGESON

Money-Back Guarantee If You Are Not Satisfied

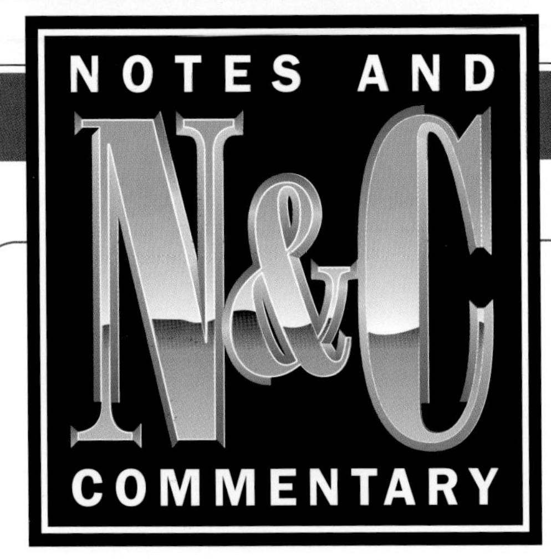

VOLUME 47 NO. 1

CONTACTING AQ

Automobile Quarterly, ISSN 0005-1438, ISBN 1-59613-053-9 (978-1-59613-053-1), is published quarterly by Automobile Heritage Publishing and Communications, LLC. Editorial and publication offices: 800 East 8th Street, New Albany, Indiana, USA 47150. Telephone (812) 948-AUTO (2886); fax (812) 948-2816; e-mail info@autoquarterly.com; Web site www.autoquarterly.com.

SUBSCRIPTION SERVICE

For subscriptions, back issues, indexes, reader service, changes of address, and order entry, call (866) 838-2886. If calling from Indiana or outside the U.S., call (812) 948-2886. Back issue prices start at $25.95, plus shipping. For domestic subscription orders: 1 year (4 issues), $79.95; 2 years (8 issues), $149.95; 3 years (12 issues), $199.95. for Canadian orders: 1 year, $99.95; 2 years, $189.95; 3 years, $259.95. For all other international orders: 1 year, $109.95; 2 years, $209.95; 3 years, $289.95. Mastercard, Visa, or American Express are accepted. Order online at www.autoquarterly.com. To order by mail, please send check or money order to ***AQ/ Automobile Quarterly***, Subscriber Services, P.O. Box 334, Stafford, TX 77497. The fax number for orders is (812) 948-2816.

POSTMASTER

Please send all changes of address to: ***Automobile Quarterly***, P.O. Box 1950, New Albany, IN 47151. Periodical postage paid at New Albany, Indiana, and at additional mailing offices.

LEGAL NOTICE

OPPORTUNITY

Details of fund raising programs for car clubs and automobile museums are available by calling: (812) 948-AUTO (2886).

Cover & Contents

Art by Niles Nakaoka.

Frontispiece

Color photography: p.1, courtesy of the Automotive Hall of Fame.

LaSalle

This story about LaSalle was excerpted from "Cadillac: Standard of the World." Work is underway by the AQ staff to produce a completely updated edition of this award-winning history. For photography sourcing, thanks to Mary Ellen Loscar and Ron McQueeny from IMS Photo, and John Kyros from GM Media Archive for their assistance.

Black-and-white photography: pp, 6, 7, 8, 10, 11 from the AQ Photo and Research Archives; p. 14 from IMS Photo.

Color photography: pp. 4-5, 9-13, 15, 16, 18, 19 from the AQ Photo and Research Archives; pp. 6, 7, 17 courtesy of GM Media Archive.

G-Modified Racing Revolution

One of the reasons why technology accelerated so rapidly in the 1100cc class is that all of the major de-

(continued on page 120)

Welcome to
KEENELAND
Information
Grandstand
SOUTH
4th Annual
KEENELAND
CONCOURS
d'ELEGANCE
AUGUST 23-26, 2007
Lexington, Kentucky
Please join us for this unique four-day event presenting the best o
the bluegrass and featuring hundreds of exquisite automobiles on t
historic grounds of the Keeneland Race Course.
2007 Marque Car: Jaguar
keenelandconcours.com 859-422-3329
All proceeds benefit The Kentucky Children's Hospital and WUKY public radio

velopers were also good racing drivers. Even before the English cars came, Renato Ambrosini of Siata was the 750cc champion of Italy and Ilario Bandini was the 1100cc champion. Then, John Cooper was the FIII Champion of England and Elva's Frank Nichols successfully raced a Lotus VI and a sports racing special at Goodwood. With The Broadley Special, built by his brother Graham and himself, Lola's Eric Broadley won the major trophy of the 750 Motor Club. The best driver among the English constructors was Colin Chapman. At Goodwood in May of 1956 he beat World Champion Mike Hawthorn, both in Lotus Elevens. The Cooper team was so complete it even had a team dog, a friendly mongrel named "Boxer," whom John Cooper once photographed at the wheel of one of the FIII cars. Among the Americans, Gerry Mong was an accomplished driver with a national championship in H-Modified driving his own car in 1965 ARRC at Daytona. He also drove a G-Modified 1100cc Alfa-engined Bobsy in the 1966 ARRC at Riverside but was beaten by a Cosworth-engined Bourgeault that, he recalls, "would go like the dickens down the back straight."

This article could not have been written without the help of Alix Lafontant, Pat Lafontant, Joe Brown, Georgia Brown, Tom Saal, Chuck Dietrich, Jane Dietrich, Frank Nichols, Ray Boldt, Warren Ballard, Jim Eichenlaub, Stanley Rosenthal, Henry Wessells, Art Brow, Reed Andrews, David Gardner, Larry Berman, Sports Car Club of America, Paul Richards, Philippe Defechereux, Pete Lyons, Doug Nye, Ken Breslauer, Chuck Krueger, John de Boer, Otto Linton, Frank Dominianni, Luigi Chinetti Jr., Frank Bott, Ed Hugus, Dott. Dino Bandini, Franco Verni , Pete Vack, George Jasberg, Pat Dennis, Max Goldman, Dave Fenton, Richard Gent, Jr., John Cooper, Paul Richards, Lex DuPont, George Alderman, David Cooper, Burdette Martin, Suzy Dietrich, M.R.J. Wylie, Peg Wylie, Gerry Mong, Kaye Hier, Alan Hier, Peter Sachs, Bill Bradley, Scott Bradley, Art Eastman, Jeff Allison, International Motor Racing Research Center, Bill Green, Mark Steigerwald, and Cameron Argetsinger.

Black-and-white photography: pp, 20, 25 (top right), 27 (bottom left and right), 29 (right) from the collection of Chuck and Jane Dietrich; pp. 22, 24, 26 (right) courtesy of Joe Brown; p. 23 by Warren Ballard, from the collection of Jim Eichenlaub; pp. 25 (top left, bottom), 26 (top left), 27 (top) courtesy of Alix Lafontant; p. 28 (top left) from the collection of Dave Fenton; p. 28 (top right, bottom left) from the collection of Reed Andrews; p. 28 (bottom right) by Ray Boldt.

Color photography: pp. 21, 24 courtesy of Joe Brown; p. 26 from the collection of Chuck and Jane Dietrich; p. 29 courtesy of Alix Lafontant.

Bibliography

Breslauer, Ken. *12 Hours of Sebring*. Auto Racing Memories, St. Petersburg, Fla. 1987;

Defechereux, Philippe. *Watkins Glen 1948 – 1952*. Beeman Jorgensen Inc., Indianapolis, 1998;

Donick, Jim. *Vintage Sports Car*. VSCCA, Pleasant Valley, NY, Issue Number 5, 2005;

Franco Fabbri and Cesare Sangiorgi. *Bandini*. Dott. Dino Bandini, Regsitro Automobile Storiche Italiano, Forli, Italy, 2004;

Lyons, Pete. *Can – Am*. Motorbooks International, Osceola, Wisc., 1995;

Nye, Doug. *Cooper Cars*. Osprey Publishing Ltd., London, England 1983.

Sands of Time

As mentioned in the introduction of this story, Fred Booth was the "eyes on the beach" for the *Daytona Beach News-Journal* for decades. His memories of racing on the sands of Daytona spanned 50 years, and he was acquainted with several drivers who raced there, including Tommy Milton, Ralph DePalma and many other familiar names. His notes on the record runs and the formation of the Daytona International Speedway exist in the AQ Photo and Research Archives.

Black-and-white photography: pp. 30, 35 (top), 36 (bottom), 37, 38, 39, 43 from the Beaulieu National Motor Museum's Motoring Picture Library; p. 32 (bottom) courtesy of GM Media Archives; p. 32 (top) from LAT Photographic; pp. 33, 34, 35 (bottom), 36 (top), 40, 42 from the AQ Photo and Research Archives.

All color photography from the Beaulieu National Motor Museum's Motoring Picture Library.

Automotive Hall of Fame

Special thanks go out to Jeffrey Leestma for allowing us time for interviews and follow up. In their quest to honor and memorialize the heroes of the industry, the executives, board and staff of the Automotive Hall of Fame have become heroes—and heroines—in their own right.

All photography courtesy of the Automotive Hall of Fame.

(continued on page 122)

1ST INTERNATIONAL CAR DESIGN EXPOFORUM
TURIN - OVAL MAY, FROM 21 TO 25, 2008

DRIVING AHEAD

Contact Information
Automotive Hall of Fame
21400 Oakwood Boulevard
Dearborn, MI 48124
Phone: 313-240-4000
Fax: 313-240-8641
Web site: www.automotivehalloffame.org

Around the World in a Skoda

The author is editor at Classique Car Library. Thanks to the Skoda Club and Bret Prochazka for the preparation of this little-known story.

Black-and-white photography: p54 courtesy of Skoda Auto, Corporate Historical Archives; pp. 55-59 courtesy of Bret Prochazka.

Nurburgring

This story is posthumously published and in honor of Randy Barnett, who died Jan. 13, 2007. Randy had a special fondness for the Ring. As his former *Stars and Stripes* co-worker Mike Spear noted in his rememberances: "Randy loved the Nurburgring and had run that circuit at speed many times, but maybe his most memorable was as a passenger in an Opel sedan with Jackie Stewart at the wheel. It wasn't the speed that made it memorable, although that was a factor; it was the way Stewart's driving skills enabled him to root out those Porsche and BMW drivers going through the curves. 'They couldn't believe it when our Opel passed them,' Randy said with a laugh. 'They had no idea Stewart was driving.'"

Randy retired from his 25-year motor sports editor post at *Stars and Stripes* in 1991, when he and his wife moved from Germany to Clarksville, Ind. His work brought him into close contact with racing greats such as Stirling Moss, Nikki Lauda and Ayrton Senna, and family friends include the Argetsingers of Watkins Glen. He was on staff at AQ as copy editor and contributor during 2001-03, a period for which we feel fortunate to have known him.

Black-and-white photography: p. 62 (left), from the Beaulieu National Motor Museum's Motoring Picture Library; pp. 62 (right), 65, 67 from LAT Photographic; pp. 63, 64, 66 courtesy of Ford Motor Co. and Wieck Media Services, Inc.

Color photography: p. 60 (satellite image) copyright Google Earth, illustration copyright Europa Technologies and GeoContent (2006); p. 61 from the Beaulieu National Motor Museum's Motoring Picture Library; p. 66 courtesy of Ford Motor Co. and Wieck Media Services, Inc.; pp. 67, 69 (right) from LAT Photographic; pp. 68-69 (left) courtesy of GM Media Archives.

Jon Shirley's Garage

For letting us have a peek inside his immaculate garage, the editors are grateful to Jon Shirley, a collector who comfortably fits into the "serious enthusiast" classification.

Color photography by Phil Berg.

Art Gallery with Niles Nakaoka

Mahalo to this issue's artist for his time and talents. His self-taught skills at watercolor and mixed media has given the world many treasures. The open-wheel excitement that is Formula 1 racing comes through the canvas in the most breathtaking ways.

All photography courtesy of Niles Nakaoka.

Contact Information
Niles Nakaoka
284-R Mananai Place
Honolulu, HI 96818
Phone: 808-487-4009
E-mail: nilestyleart@yahoo.com
Web site: www.nilesnakaoka.com

The Ascent of the Auburn

All photography from the AQ Photo and Research Archives.

Capturing an Era

References:
Portrait of a Decade: F. Jack Hurley
Roy Stryker: U.S.A., 1943-1950: Steven W. Plattner

Photographers:
Charlotte Brooks: p. 112
Esther Bubley: pp. 109, 112
Harold Corsini: pp. 108, 109, 111
Sol Libsohn: p. 110
Edwin & Louise Rosskam: p. 109
Charles Rotkin: p. 112
John Vachoni: p. 110
Todd Webb: p. 109

We appreciate the efforts and information furnished by Mr. Bill Carner, Photo Archives, Special Collections Ekstrom Library, University of Louisville, Louisville, Kentucky.

Notes and Commentary

We wish to thank Pat Cole at JMPR Public Relations for his help with our obituary on Bob Petersen, and Teresa Barnett for her help with our dedication to Randy, her late husband.

Coda

Photography courtesy of IWM/Camera Press/Retna.

Back Cover

Debossment of the Auburn emblem from the AQ Photo and Research Archives.

Changes, Updates & Eratta

In AQ Volume 46 Number 3, p. 51 of "The Dynasty of Design" the erroneous caption for the top photo names Irv Rybicki with Harley Earl. It is, in fact, George Jergenson with Earl. Ken Bowes, a Toronto-based industrial designer and Art Center grad, correctly identified Jergenson, who went on to chair the Industrial Design department at Art Center.

Digital glitches got our goad in Vols. 46-3 and 46-4, in our Cord and Duesenberg stories, respectively. Some of the photos in those stories were "flipped" and went to press unaltered. We believe we have killed the gremlins.

Robert E. Petersen, Founder of *Hot Rod*, *Motor Trend* Magazines and Benefactor of the Petersen Automotive Museum Passes On at 80

Robert E. Petersen, an entrepreneur who single-handedly created the largest special-interest publishing company in America, was instrumental in the evolution of the hot-rodding culture, and who, with his wife Margie, realized his dream of establishing an educational museum to pay tribute to the automobile, died on Friday, March 23, 2007 at St. John's Hospital in Santa Monica, Calif., after a short but valiant battle with neuroendocrine cancer. He was 80.

"Mr. Petersen helped create and feed the American obsession with the automobile, delivering gasoline-powered dreams to the mailboxes of millions," said Dick Messer, director of the Petersen Automotive Museum in Los Angeles. "He understood the thrill that an average person could get from seeing and reading about horsepower as an art form."

A native of Southern California, Petersen's mother passed away when he was 10, leaving him with his Danish-immigrant father, who worked as a truck and equipment mechanic. As a young man he picked up his father's skills, learning to weld, de-coke engines, and hone his fascination with cars.

After graduating from Barstow High School in the mid-1940s, he moved to Los Angeles, working at MGM studios as a messenger boy. Following service in the Army Air Corps toward the end of Word War II, Petersen, now an independent publicist immersed in the burgeoning customized auto culture of California, was instrumental in creating the first hot-rod show at the Los Angeles Armory. To help establish the event, in January 1948 he launched *Hot Rod Magazine*, and hawked the magazine at local speedways for 25 cents a copy. *Motor Trend*, a more upscale publication for production car enthusiasts, and dozens of other titles aimed at specialty automotive segments soon followed.

Petersen spent decades as Chairman of the Board of Petersen Publishing Company, which was at one time America's leading publisher of special-interest consumer magazines and books before its sale to private investors in August 1996. Among its other diverse successful titles are *Teen*, *Sport*, *Rod & Custom*, and *Guns & Ammo*. He also headed a wide variety of other businesses including ammunition manufacturing, real estate development and aviation services that each reflected another passion he shared.

Firmly established as an American success story, Petersen had one lasting vision: an educational museum to pay tribute to the automobile. On June 11, 1994, the lifelong dream of Robert E. Petersen was fulfilled with the opening of a 300,000-square-foot automotive museum named in his honor, made possible by his $30 million endowment.

Today the Petersen Automotive Museum in Los Angeles stands as the nation's premiere automotive museum, serving thousands of visitors each year. Its mission remains to educate and excite generations of auto enthusiasts with the fascinating stories, vehicles and people that have influenced the American love affair with the automobile – a mission that has been a resounding success thanks to the generosity of its main benefactor.

In addition to his noted auto collection, Petersen also developed a keen interest in sport shooting. He served as shooting sports commissioner for the 1984 Los Angeles Olympic Games, where he was responsible for building that venue from an old dairy farm within six months.

Petersen served as president and chairman of the board of the Boys' and Girls' Club of Hollywood, and was a member of the National Board of Directors for the Boys' and Girls' Club of America. He was active in support of numerous children's charities and also served as a member of the Los Angeles City Library Commission.

Both he and his wife have been major contributors to the Music Center of Los Angeles and the Los Angeles County Museum of Art. Additionally, he was a founding member of the Thalians social society, which raises money for the Mental Health Center at Cedars-Sinai Medical Center. His ongoing contributions to the community earned him numerous special citations from the Los Angeles County Board of Supervisors and Los Angeles City Council.

Petersen was to be honored with both the "Automotive Icon" and "Visionary" awards at the Petersen museum's annual gala on May 10. The ceremony will now be held as a tribute to Mr. Petersen and his contributions to the institution and community.

"What made him so special was that he gave every ounce of his energy and abilities to his dreams. He was a quiet man who truly became an American icon," the Petersen museum's Messer said. "He made his living doing things he loved and he found success at every turn. The way he lived his life, always looking for ways to give back in return for the success he enjoyed, made you proud to count him as a friend. The museum is now his legacy."

He is survived by his wife Margie.

ROYALTY AT THE WHEEL

It was a dark hour for Great Britain. The country had been at war with Germany since September 1939. Princess Elizabeth, who was 13 years old when war broke out, was evacuated with her younger sister, Princess Margaret, to Windsor Castle, Berkshire. For years, its citizenry was subjected to relentless Luftwaffe bombings, and in June 1944 German V-1 "buzz bombs" started to pound the island nation, day and night, fair weather and foul.

In early 1945, a concerned Elizabeth approached her father, the king, and asked that she be allowed to contribute directly to the war effort. *Time* magazine, in their March 12 edition, reported: "Princess Elizabeth was commissioned an honorary second subaltern in the ATS (Auxiliary Territorial Service, Britain's WAC) [and] started full-time training in southern England." Indeed so; the princess was known as No. 230873, Second Subaltern Elizabeth Windsor and was primarily trained as a driver, which included instruction in basic motor mechanics as well as the proper care and keeping of motor vehicles.

Second Subaltern Elizabeth Windsor was the first and, so far, the only female member of the royal family to actually serve in the armed forces. In a time of dark despair, the beautiful little princess, who would later become queen, rose to the occasion to inspire and give comfort to her fellow countrymen. It was a moment at which the world could be proud and truly one of England's finest hours. AQ